"The Latin phrase *nota bene* (n.b.) means 'note well!' Sr. Melannie Svoboda not only knows that phrase—she lives it. In *Gracious Goodness* we have fifty-two n.b.'s that will enrich our spiritual treasure troves."

—Bishop Robert Morneau, Auxiliary Bishop of Green Bay

"In *Gracious Goodness*, Sr. Melannie Svoboda offers accessible meditations to today's Everyman and Everywoman. These meditations come from life's daily gifts and they range from kindness to whimsy. Anyone who wants a spiritual companion for the new millennium could do no better than to turn these pages."

—William J. Bausch, author, *The Yellow Brick Road:*
A Storyteller's Approach to the Spiritual Journey

"Sr. Melannie herself is one of God's treasures as she so ably demonstrates here. She delights us, encourages us, and surprises us with her inspiring insights and homey images. A wonderful book!"

—Gwen Costello, author, *A Prayer Primer for Catechists and Teachers*

"We are once again indebted to Sr. Melannie Svoboda for opening our eyes to the beauty of life. Prophet-like, she guides us in fifty-two brief essays, from Abundance to Zeal, to consider the Spirit's gifts and qualities with fresh insight, with a new slant. She peppers the chapters with stories, poignant quotations, and references to Jesus' words and example."

—John van Bemmel, author, *Prayers about Everyday Stuff*,
coauthor, *100 Prayers for Making Faith Connections*

Gracious Goodness

Gracious Goodness

Living Each Day in the Gifts of the Spirit

MELANNIE SVOBODA, SND

LOYOLA PRESS.
A JESUIT MINISTRY
CHICAGO

LOYOLA PRESS.
A JESUIT MINISTRY
3441 N. ASHLAND AVENUE
CHICAGO, ILLINOIS 60657
(800) 621-1008
WWW.LOYOLAPRESS.ORG

A previous edition of this book was published as *Abundant Treasures: Meditations on the Many Gifts of the Spirit* (Mystic, CT: Twenty-Third Publications, 2000).

Cover photo Getty Images/Nick Daly
Cover design by Judine O'Shea
Interior design by Maggie Hong

Library of Congress Cataloging-in-Publication Data
Svoboda, Melannie.
  Gracious goodness : living each day in the gifts of the spirit / Melannie Svoboda.
    p. cm.
  Rev. ed. of: Abundant treasures. 2000.
  Includes bibliographical references.
  ISBN-13: 978-0-8294-2719-6
  ISBN-10: 0-8294-2719-8
  1. Christian life—Catholic authors. 2. Spiritual life—Catholic Church. I. Svoboda,
Melannie. Abundant treasures. II. Title.
  BX2350.3.S86 2008
  248.4--dc22

                                                                           2008000641

Printed in the United States of America
08 09 10 11 12 13 Versa 10 9 8 7 6 5 4 3 2 1

To Kathleen (Kay) Koehler: From the day we met on the playground at St. Felicitas School over forty years ago, you have been a gift of the Spirit in my life.

Contents

Introduction

Dear Reader:

This is a book on the gifts of the Holy Spirit. But I use the word "gifts" in a broad sense. I include the traditional seven gifts of the Holy Spirit, but I also include other gifts such as attentiveness, beauty, diversity, intimacy, leadership, and patience. The book even includes some gifts of the Spirit not always thought of as gifts: bereavement, common sense, death, desire, guilt, failure, relaxation, and levity.

The fifty-two gifts are arranged in alphabetical order with the exception of the last selection: death. I've placed death at the end of the book since death is, in a way, the last gift, the final gift, the ultimate gift.

Each chapter begins with an appropriate quotation from a wide variety of sources followed by a meditation on the particular gift, a meditation rooted in both Scripture and daily life. At the end of each meditation there are one or more questions to facilitate personal reflection on that gift in your own life. And finally, each chapter concludes with a short prayer to encourage your prayerful dialogue with God about each gift.

I call this book *Gracious Goodness*, for the gifts of the Holy Spirit are given to us by a God whose goodness knows no bounds. How blessed are we to be the recipients of these gracious gifts.

May this small book help you to discover the grace, goodness, and surprising diversity of the Holy Spirit's gifts in your own life.

O Lord, it is you who are my portion and my cup;
It is you yourself who are my prize.
The lot marked out for me is my delight:
Welcome indeed the heritage that falls to me!

(PSALM 16:5–6)

Gracious Goodness

1 On Abundance

We have all benefited from the rich blessings he brought to us—
blessing upon blessing heaped upon us.
—John 1:16

Astronomers tell us there are between 50 billion and 100 billion stars in our galaxy. (One billion is 1,000 million.) What's more, there are an estimated 50 billion galaxies in the universe (the known universe, that is). That means, if every galaxy has 50 billion stars (a conservative estimate), then there are 50 billion times 50 billion stars swirling around in space—that is, 2,500,000,000,000,000,000,000 stars. That is a heck of a lot of stars!

From the sheer number of stars alone, it is pretty obvious: Our God is a God of abundance. It seems that when it came to creating stars, at least, God got carried away. God couldn't stop with two or three or even a few dozen stars—as reasonableness would dictate. No, God had to keep churning them out, star after star after star. And it is not just with stars that God got carried away. The numbers are just as mind-boggling when it comes to other things God made—like grains of sand, snowflakes, orchids, bees.

> We are meant to love abundantly—just as God loves—with sweeping gestures, to the max, as if there were no tomorrow.

God's apparent lack of restraint when it comes to creating things is but a symptom of a deeper "problem": God lacks restraint when it comes to loving, too. In fact, God is most unrestrained when it comes to loving. Put another way, God cannot love except abundantly.

Isn't that what Jesus was all about? Jesus' life was one big show-and-tell of God's abundant love. What is the parable of the prodigal son, for example, but a proclamation of the abundance of God's love? What is Jesus' agony in the garden but a graphic demonstration that, when all is lost and nothing makes any sense any more, the only proper thing to do is to fall backwards into the arms of the God of Abundant Love—and trust, trust, trust. We are meant to love abundantly—just as God loves—with sweeping gestures, to the max, as if there were no tomorrow.

In her book *The Writing Life*, Annie Dillard says: "One of the few things I know about writing is this: spend it all, shoot it, play it, lose it, all, right away, every time. Do not hoard what seems good for a later place in the book, or for another book; give it, give it all, give it now. . . . Anything you do not give freely and abundantly becomes lost to you. You open your safe and find ashes."

Good advice for writing, great advice for loving.

How have I experienced the abundance of God's love in my life? What hinders me from loving more abundantly? What helps me?

Spirit of Jesus, fill me with your abundant love.

2 On Anger

If we had been better people, we would have been angrier oftener.
—Richard Bentley

Anger gets a lot of bad press these days—especially in religious circles. For many people, anger is a negative emotion, a shameful thing. After all, anger makes individuals speak hurtful words, scream profanities, throw dishes, brandish baseball bats, and even kill.

That may be true. Sometimes. But sometimes anger can be good. It can even be a gift of the Spirit. Just look at Jesus. He got angry. Remember how he cleansed the Temple?

Even the phrase "cleansed the Temple" is a euphemism—as if Jesus strolled in with a little plastic pail and began to mop the corridors or something. Not so. When Jesus cleansed the temple, he stormed up the steps like a madman, waving a whip around his head. He screamed at the moneychangers while hurling their tables and chairs.

Some people are quick to say, "But it was okay for Jesus to get angry. After all, he was God." Others excuse his anger by saying, "His anger was justified." The truth is, many of us are uncomfortable with, or even embarrassed by, this image of a raging, quasi-maniacal Jesus. We prefer a gentler Jesus, the Good-Shepherd-cuddling-a-white-wooly-lamb Jesus. But we must be honest: the raging Jesus is just as real as the cuddling Jesus. And sooner or later we must come to accept this anger in Jesus—as well as the anger in ourselves. We must see how, at times, anger is the only fitting response to a situation. Anger can be a friend.

Anger is our friend when it shakes us out of our complacency. There is an innate tendency in many of us to let things be, to not rock the boat, to keep things just as they are—no matter how ridiculous, awful, or unjust. That is where anger can come in. If we spot something that is not right, our spontaneous anger might just be the spark we need to act; that is, to do something about making things right, or at least better.

Anger is our friend when it draws our attention to something that may be wrong within ourselves. Sometimes our anger is a red flag, alerting us to a deeper problem we may be avoiding. Persistent anger can be a way of cloaking other emotions that might be too painful for us to name, let alone deal with—emotions such as hurt, grief, loneliness, or fear. When we are angry, then, it makes sense not to dismiss our anger immediately. Rather, we might want to sit with our anger for a while, walk around it, and explore its roots. We might be surprised at what we discover.

There is a point where patience ceases to be a virtue and a point where anger becomes one.

A few years back I found myself complaining to my spiritual director about a particular situation in my life. Month after month, I complained—with considerable anger. Then one day I said to her, "You know, I'm sick and tired of hearing myself complain about this thing." (No doubt she was, too!) Then I found myself saying, "I guess I'd better either do something about this thing, or shut up already!" My anger eventually led me to take some definite steps, albeit difficult steps, to better the situation I was in. There is a point where patience ceases to be a virtue and a point where anger becomes one.

What makes me angry? Have I ever sat with my anger, walked around it, or explored its roots? If so, what did I find?

Jesus, you got angry too. Help me to befriend my anger, so that it may lead me to work more actively for the coming of your kingdom.

3 On Attentiveness

To pay attention, this is our endless and proper work.
—Mary Oliver

There's an old joke about a farmer who bought a mule that was supposed to listen to whatever it was told to do. The farmer told the mule to pull his plow, but the mule refused to budge. The farmer yelled at the beast, pleaded with him, cajoled him, but to no avail. Frustrated, the man called the previous owner to come over. "I thought you said this mule listened to whatever you told him to do," he complained. "But he won't listen to me." Without saying a word, the former owner walked away and returned with a big stick. He took the stick and swatted the mule once across the rear end. Immediately the mule began to pull the farmer's plow. "See?" said the man, "He listens real good. But first you've got to get his attention."

The word *attention* is an interesting word. Did you ever notice that, in English at least, we say pay attention? Ordinarily we don't say do attention or even give attention. Certainly we never say loan attention. No, attention is something we pay. The verb *pay* implies that every time we focus our attention on someone or something, we pay a price.

And we do pay a price—our time and energy, both of which are very valuable. They are also limited. Consequently, we cannot pay attention to everything that clamors for our attention on a given day or we would go insane. No, we have to be selective in what we pay attention to.

The ability to be attentive is a gift. It is also essential for salvation.

Jesus knew this. Although he may never have yelled, "Pay attention!" he did say, "Behold!" on a number of occasions. "Behold the lilies." "Behold this child." "Behold that poor widow putting in those two coins." "Behold, I make all things new." Jesus' "behold" was his way of saying, "Pay attention now! This is really important!" In fact, Jesus' entire life was bent on directing our attention, focusing our time and energy on the things that really matter in life: the love God has for us, the love we should have for each other, our personal relationship with God in prayer, and heeding the cry of the poor. *In other words, the things necessary for salvation.* Salvation begins with attentiveness to the things that really count.

Salvation begins with attentiveness to the things that really count.

Who or what is getting my attention these days? Do I know what the priorities are in my life?

God, help me to be attentive today to the things that really matter.

4 On Availability

God does not ask for our ability or our inability, but for our availability.

—Anonymous

Years ago I took an Old Testament course with a professor who made the Scriptures come alive. I still remember the day he did a dramatic reading of the call of the prophet Isaiah (Isaiah 6:1–8). He explained that Isaiah was praying in the temple one day when he had a vision of God—complete with singing angels, a scary earthquake, and lots of billowing smoke. Realizing he had seen God, Isaiah was overwhelmed with the sense of his own sinfulness. As he cowered in a corner, one of the angels came to him and touched his lips with a burning coal, thus purifying him of his sin.

It was then that Isaiah overheard God asking himself, "Whom shall I send to speak to my people? Who shall be my prophet?" After my professor spoke those words, he became Isaiah. Rising slowly from his desk, he pointed dramatically to his chest and cried out, "Here I am! Send me!" That image of Isaiah volunteering to be God's prophet has stayed with me all these years. It is a stunning example of availability.

Availability is the gift of the Spirit, which enables us to offer ourselves to God. It means we place our time, talents, and energy at God's disposal. Availability is not easy. Why? First, when we volunteer ourselves to God, we never know what we're getting into. Availability is like handing God a blank check. We don't know what amount God is going to fill in. Little wonder we balk.

Availability is also difficult because it often involves changing our plans—and if there's one thing we like, it's making plans. It is fine to make plans, of course, as long as we remain open to change.

What can hinder availability to God? Fear. Instead of saying, "Here I am, God!" we may say, "But I've never done anything like that before" or "I feel so inadequate to the task."

> *Availability is the gift of the Spirit, which enables us to offer ourselves to God.*

At such times we should remember: if God is truly asking us to do this thing, then God will give us the graces we need to do it—or the graces we need to accept failure if we can't do it.

Jesus was totally available to God. In Gethsemane he said, "Not my will, but yours be done." In other words, "Here I am, God! Send me!"

How do I make myself available to God? What hinders me from greater availability?

Here I am, God! Send me!

5 On Beauty

Of all psychology's sins, the most mortal is its neglect of beauty.
—James Hillman

Two old friends were walking down the road one evening when they began to argue. As they went along, they shouted at one another as each tried to impose his view upon the other. Suddenly, one of them caught sight of the setting sun. He pointed it out to his friend. Immediately the men ceased their arguing. They stood side by side in silence, gazing in wonder and awe at the beauty of the sunset. When the sun had slipped beneath the horizon, the two friends started on their way again. Only now, having forgotten what they had been arguing about, they walked together cheerfully and at peace with one another.

This story reminds us that beauty has the power to heal. Unfortunately, this healing power is not always recognized in our technological society. This fact is reflected even in the curricula of many of our schools. If educational budgets are cut, what goes first? Not science. Not math. Not even sports. No, the arts go first. Such thinking implies that the arts are dispensable. Beauty is something we can live without.

But is beauty dispensable? Thomas Moore, in his classic book *Care of the Soul*, argues that beauty is absolutely essential for the health of the soul. In fact, he goes so far as to say that if we lack beauty in our lives, we will probably suffer from familiar disturbances such as depression, paranoia, meaninglessness, and addiction. Moore writes, "The soul craves beauty, and in its absence suffers what James Hillman has called 'beauty neurosis.'" The psychologist Carl Jung, also a believer in the power of beauty, once suggested to a colleague, "Why not go out into the forest for a time, literally? Sometimes a tree tells you more than you can read in books."

Christianity at its best has always understood and appreciated the power of beauty to nourish the soul. Just look at our ancient cathedrals, with their stained glass windows and soaring spires, our solemn liturgies with their chants and incense. Just listen to the strains of Franz Schubert's "Ave Maria" or behold Michelangelo's *Pieta*. Just read the poetry of St. John of the Cross or the prose of St. Teresa of Ávila.

Jesus was remarkably attentive to the beauty in his everyday life. He appreciated, for example, the beauty in nature. The Gospels show him attuned to the weather patterns and changing seasons of his native land. He knew his trees, noticed flowers, and was even something of a bird watcher. Jesus also observed animals and often used them very effectively in his teachings.

Jesus appreciated beauty in other forms, too. The son of a carpenter, he probably knew wood very well and had an eye for color, line, and texture. The son of a homemaker, he was well acquainted with the beauty of freshly baked bread, a carefully sewn garment, and good wine.

But most of all, Jesus was attentive to the beauty of human love. He experienced love firsthand from his parents. Later, he encountered it in the men and women who were so devoted to him. Throughout his ministry, Jesus marveled at love's power to do incredibly beautiful things. Jesus' experience of human love made it easier for him to believe in the love that God, Abba, had for him. Beauty is a gift of the Spirit that nourishes and heals our souls, for ultimately, Beauty is but another name for God.

> *Beauty is a gift of the Spirit that nourishes and heals our souls, for ultimately, Beauty is but another name for God.*

How do I make time for beauty in my life? Have I ever experienced beauty's healing power?

Beauty, ever ancient and ever new, please nourish and heal my soul today.

6 On Bereavement

Those who live in the Lord never see each other for the last time.
—German proverb

The word *bereavement* means to be stripped, to be deprived of something, usually through death. The word comes from the Old English words *be* and *reafian*, meaning "to be robbed." Grief is the emotional suffering that bereavement causes. If this is what bereavement and grief mean, then how in heaven's name can they be considered gifts of the Spirit? I will get to that. But first, here is what I know about bereavement and grief.

Bereavement cannot be measured, yet we are forever trying to measure it. A friend of mine was burying her ninety-four-year-old father, who had lived with her the last three years of his life. At the wake I overheard someone say to her, "But Ruthie, you had him so long!"—implying that the pain of Ruth's grief should be lessened by that fact. Ruth's response was a good one. She cried, "I know, I know. But that's what makes this even harder, because every day he gave me another reason to love him!"

Who can measure the pain of bereavement? Who can compare one person's grief to another's? And yet we try always to make a comparison. We say things like, "But my husband was so young," as if losing an elderly husband is easier. "But he was my only son," as if losing one son when you have two is less painful. "She was taken from me so quickly," as if watching a loved one die slowly and painfully is much better. Or we try to convince ourselves that our grief isn't really that bad after all, thank you. We say foolish things like, "I know I'll get over this." "After all, I did have fifty-two years with her." "At least he's not suffering anymore." These are all attempts to reduce the agony, to diminish the pain. But they seldom work.

Grief is grief. It is not despair. It is not hunger. It is not paralysis. It is not fear. Although sometimes it can feel like all of these things, no, grief is grief. It is unlike anything else in the world. C. S. Lewis describes this so well in his poignant book *A Grief Observed*, a journal he wrote after the death of his wife. He says that grief "is not local"—that is, restricted to one place. No, he feels his wife's absence everywhere: "Her absence is like the sky, spread over everything."

Death is not the only thing we grieve. Any loss can make us grieve: the loss of a job, a relationship, our hair, our eyesight, a cherished idea, a favorite place, an accustomed way of doing things, our youth. When we are grieving over the death of a loved one, people take notice, they understand. They go out of their way to offer their condolences. But when we are grieving things like the loss of a breast or our independence, sometimes we stand alone.

How is bereavement a gift of the Spirit? It is the underside of love, goodness, and meaning. We grieve because we have loved and have been loved. It is as simple as that. Perhaps there is no clearer proof of love's greatness than the pain we feel when the object of our love is taken from us. Grief also underscores the essential goodness and meaningfulness of life. If people were not good and things did not matter, we would never grieve. But people are good, things do count, and life does have meaning. That is grief's protest. That is also grief's promise.

> We grieve because we have loved and have been loved.

What has been my experience with grief and bereavement?

Jesus, Risen Lord, in my grieving I cling to your promise of everlasting love.

7 On Childlikeness

A teacher told the story of the Good Samaritan to her class and asked, "What does this story teach you?" Said one child, "When I'm in trouble, someone should help me!"

When Jesus was asked to point to someone who epitomized the qualities he was looking for in his disciples, he didn't go to a palace, synagogue, or marketplace. No, he went to a playground. There, calling over to himself a little girl, he put his arm around her shoulders and said to his disciples, "This is the kind of person I want you to become. She has the qualities I'm looking for."

We can only begin to imagine the shock of his disciples as they sputtered, "Her?! A little kid?! This is a joke, right?" The disciples had every reason to be shocked. They protested, "But Jesus, children are ignorant, immature, self-centered, undisciplined, helpless, naughty, naive, cruel, inconsiderate, and totally irresponsible. And they have no legal rights whatsoever." In short, children were all those things the disciples, as adults, were trying so hard not to be.

But Jesus did not retract what he had said. No, he was insistent and made his point even more plain, saying, "I'm telling you, you will not enter the Kingdom of Heaven unless you become like this little kid."

We might ask, "What is it about children that make them shoo-ins for the Kingdom of God?" Here and in other passages, Jesus tells us. For one thing, children are open. They let reality in—not like so many adults who, over the years, build elaborate barriers to shield themselves against the real world. Those barriers, unfortunately, keep out not only the world—they keep out God, who can come into our lives only through that real world.

Children are trustful too. They readily take your hand. They go where you lead them. They believe what you tell them. Isn't this receptivity exactly what we need in our relationship with God? Like children, don't we have to trust God, take God's hand, go where God may lead us, and believe what God tells us?

Finally, children have no real claims on their parents' love. They do nothing to merit or earn the love that is poured out upon them from the moment they enter the world. Good parents don't love their kids because they have to. They love their kids because they love their kids. The love of a parent for a child is a lot like God's love for us.

Like children, don't we have to trust God, take God's hand, go where God may lead us, and believe what God tells us?

How childlike am I? Whom do I love as God loves?

God, you who are Father, you who are Mother, give me the heart of a child.

8 On Commitment

Make of your life something beautiful for God.
—Blessed Mother Teresa

My parents were married for sixty-five years. Sometimes my father used to tease my mother by saying, "Remember, Mil, I signed the marriage license in pencil! I can still change my mind!"

Making a commitment means signing your name in ink. It means giving your word and meaning it. It means promising something today that has ramifications for tomorrow. Every commitment involves some kind of a loss. If I make a commitment to lose twenty pounds, I cannot eat everything I might want to eat. If I make a commitment to marry Patti, I will not be marrying Laura, Allison, or Veronica. If I make a commitment to become a nun, I cannot get married, too. But every commitment also involves a gain. The only reason most of us make a commitment is because we believe the gain for us outweighs the loss. The day we no longer believe that is probably the day we question or end our commitment.

Everyone makes commitments. Even selfish people do. They make a commitment to live for themselves. Some people say they never make any commitments. But even that is a commitment. Why do we make commitments? To channel our energies, to give our lives direction, and to help ourselves do those things we see as good, meaningful, and beautiful.

Jesus made a commitment. He told his disciples, "My food is to do the will of him who sent me" (John 4:34). Today we might say, "My purpose in life is to do God's will." Keeping that commitment was not easy for Jesus. During his forty days in the wilderness, for example, he was tempted by Satan to break his commitment not once, but three times. Throughout his public life, Jesus' enemies also tried to thwart his resolve with a variety of tactics: argumentation, mockery, threats. Even his closest friend Peter tried to dissuade him from keeping a commitment that was taking him to Jerusalem to die. But Jesus held fast. In Gethsemane, he reconfirms his commitment when he says to Abba, "Take this cup away from me, but not what I will but what you will" (Mark 14:36).

Jesus called his followers to make a commitment to him: "Come follow me" (Mark 1:17). It is a commitment that has to be wholehearted: "When a [merchant] finds a pearl of great price, he sells all that he has and buys it" (Matthew 13:46). It must be irrevocable: "No one who sets a hand to the plow and looks back to what was left behind is fit for the kingdom of God" (Luke 9:62). The commitment to Jesus takes precedence over all other commitments, even those to one's family. It is a commitment that will not be easy: "I am sending you like lambs in the midst of wolves" (Luke 10:3), and "Whoever does not carry his own cross and come after me cannot be my disciple" (Luke 14:27). But Jesus also assured his followers that he himself would give them the strength necessary to live out their commitment to him: "And behold, I am with you always, until the end of the age" (Matthew 28:20).

For Christians, there is ultimately only one commitment. It is the same commitment that Jesus made—to do the will of God. It is a commitment we will be tempted to live halfheartedly at times or even abandon altogether. It is one that constantly challenges us to discern God's will in our everyday lives. But if we, like Jesus, hold fast to this commitment to the end, our joy will know no bounds (John 16:24).

> *For Christians, there is ultimately only one commitment. It is the same commitment that Jesus made—to do the will of God.*

How strong is my commitment to Jesus? How are my other commitments helping me to keep this essential one?

Jesus, help me to live my commitments today with greater trust in your strength.

9 On Common Sense

A great wisdom it is, indeed, to go mad, out of one's mind with the love of God.

—Blessed Jacopone da Todi

What, exactly, is common sense? It is hard to define. I was tempted to say that common sense tells you what common sense is, but that's not fair. So even though I am not going to define common sense, I will describe some of its characteristics. Common sense is not something we are born with; it is something we garner along the road of life.

> Common sense is not something we are born with; it is something we garner along the road of life.

A newborn baby, for example, has no common sense whatsoever—except that it cries and sucks. But those are instincts, not common sense. No, common sense comes with experience. Adults know that we do not run across a street without looking both ways. That's common sense. But a four-year-old doesn't know that. Even a nine-year-old who may know it can, tragically, forget it when her ball rolls into the street. So there are degrees of common sense.

I am not implying, of course, that everyone gets more common sense the older they get. I know adults with little common sense and teenagers with a lot of it. Nor do individuals have equal amounts of common sense about all aspects of their life. A man might have much common sense about the stock market, for example, and no common sense when it comes to relationships.

Another characteristic of common sense is that it is unreflective. If I follow my common sense, I do not take a lot of time thinking about what to do. The paradox is, however, that although common sense is unreflective, the only way we get more of it is through reflection. This means we periodically pause and take stock of the choices our common sense has been telling us to make in order to see where those choices are leading us and what they may be teaching us.

Jesus advocated common sense. He said, "If your child asks you for an egg, would you hand him a scorpion?" (Luke 11:12). No, that's not common sense. "If you set about building a house, would you build it on sand?" (Matthew 7:26–27). No, that's foolish. Jesus was implying that a lot of things that are common sense in our natural, everyday lives, are common sense for our spiritual lives as well.

Sometimes common sense in the spiritual life doesn't look like common sense. The man in the parable who sold everything to buy that unpromising field looked foolish to his neighbors. But they didn't know about the hidden treasure. Sometimes we risk all for the hidden treasure of our faith. That is real common sense!

Where is my common sense taking me these days? Has my love for Jesus ever made me do things that do not look like common sense?

Jesus, you are my treasure. Following you makes all the sense in the world.

10 On Companionship

Above all else, it seems to me,
You need some jolly company
To see life can be fun.
—Goethe

Companionship is a word rich with Eucharistic overtones. The word *companion* comes from the Latin *com*, meaning "with," and *panis*, meaning "bread." It literally means "one who breaks bread with another." Companionship began in the Garden of Eden. In the second creation account, God creates Adam first and places him in the lush garden God has prepared for him (Genesis 2:4–25). Adam has everything a man could want: loads of food, gorgeous scenery, unheard-of freedom, no boss, no deadlines, and tons of leisure time. But God detects that something is wrong. Maybe God saw Adam hanging his head and dragging his feet as he walked through the garden. Or perhaps Adam was beginning to talk to himself. Whatever abnormal behavior he was exhibiting, God spots it and diagnoses the problem: "It is not good for man to be alone," and comes up with a solution: "I will make a suitable partner for him."

So God creates the animals, but even these animals do not alleviate Adam's loneliness. That's when God comes up with an even better idea. (There are some of us who maintain that this particular idea represents the high point of creation!) God creates woman. Eve, then, is the first-ever companion.

There are some who would trace companionship back even further than the Garden of Eden—all the way back to God. I am reminded of that magnificent poem called "Creation" by the poet James Weldon Johnson. In the poem, Johnson attributes creation itself to God's need for companionship. The poem shows God stepping out into space and confessing, "I'm lonely." To ease his loneliness, God decides to "make me a world." The poem shows God fashioning the universe one day at a time. After each day's labor, God pronounces the work good, but then adds, "I'm lonely still." Eventually God creates Adam and Eve. By doing so, God's loneliness is eased, for God has found suitable companions with whom to share both life and love.

When Jesus began his public ministry, one of the first things he did was to find companions, those individuals who would share his life and ministry in a special way. Whenever Jesus faced a difficult situation, he gathered these companions around himself—sometimes all twelve, sometimes only a few. Jesus Christ, the Son of God, the Savior of the world, needed the companionship of others. Even he, as strong and powerful and good as he was, couldn't go it alone.

We can't go it alone either. We cannot face the challenges of life without the support of others. This need for companionship is one we must never be ashamed of. We must never think, "If I were more mature, I could stand on my own two feet" or "If my faith were stronger, I wouldn't have to rely so much on others." Our need for companionship, fellowship, friendship, is in the very fabric of our human psyche. It is yet one more way that we are made in the image and likeness of God.

Our need for companionship, fellowship, friendship, is in the very fabric of our human psyche.

Who accompanies me along my spiritual pathway? For whom do I provide companionship?

God, my loving companion, thank you for all those people you have given me to share my life and love.

11 On Compassion

Whatever God does, the first outburst is always compassion.
—Meister Eckhart

Throughout history, the Church—at its best—has been legendary for reaching out with compassion to the poor. The very concept of a hospital, for example, is solidly rooted in Christian compassion. Even in our own day, individuals like Dorothy Day, Frances Cabrini, John Bosco, Mother Teresa, and Henri Nouwen are known primarily for their compassion toward those in need.

Jesus was compassionate. This is the message that hits us squarely between the eyes whenever we stroll through the Gospels. There's Jesus healing the sick, giving bread to the hungry, teaching the confused, consoling the bereaved, challenging the status quo, encouraging the downcast, embracing a little child, sobbing over the death of a friend, and—perhaps most compassionately of all—forgiving the very people who tortured and executed him. Our final destiny, says Jesus in his parables, is ultimately determined by our compassion—not our humility, austerity, honesty, prayerfulness, orthodoxy, or purity. In the end, it is compassion—or the lack of it—that will separate the saved from the unsaved.

The word *compassion*, though, is easily misunderstood or misconstrued. Perhaps that is why Jesus is so absolutely clear what he means by the word. In the parable of the Last Judgment (Matthew 25:31–46), he gives example after example of not merely what compassion is, but what it does. Compassion feeds the hungry, gives drink to the thirsty, welcomes the stranger, clothes the naked, cares for the ill, and visits the imprisoned. And just to be sure we have heard what he said, Jesus repeats all six examples again at the end of the parable. If we want a gauge for our compassion, this parable provides a fine one.

Also, we must never confuse compassion with things that may look like compassion, but are not. For example, compassion is not sympathy. Sympathy says, "You poor thing!" Compassion goes beyond sympathy and says, "I am deeply moved by your plight. How may I help you?" Compassion is not obsequiousness. It never says, "If I help you, what will you do for me?"

Compassion feeds the hungry, gives drink to the thirsty, welcomes the stranger, clothes the naked, cares for the ill, and visits the imprisoned.

Finally, we must remember that compassion is a privilege. Jesus reveals himself as the compassionate one not simply because he does good works for you and me, but also because he allows us the privilege of doing good works for and through him.

What are some concrete ways I express my compassion for others?

Jesus, compassionate one, thank you for working through me today.

12 On Counsel

Discernment is the meeting point of prayer and action.
—Thomas H. Green, SJ

In his book *Surprised by the Spirit*, Father Edward Farrell notes that the gift of counsel is one of the more elusive gifts of the Spirit. He suggests, therefore, (and I agree with him) that it might be better to think of counsel in terms of discernment. What is meant by discernment? Simply put, discernment is the quest to know God's will. In what follows, I want to simply share a few thoughts on discernment that I have "discerned" over the years—from reading as well as from my own experience.

First of all, discernment is absolutely essential for our spiritual lives. One reason is because the will of God is not always obvious. Another is the fact that there are other spirits (both in ourselves and in the world around us) besides God's Spirit that can influence our choices. Most of us learned quickly in life that every movement of our hearts does not come from God. Some movements proceed from other spirits, such as selfishness ("But I want this!"), or fear ("I'm afraid to do that!"), or laziness ("I wanna stay put!"). Similarly, we know that every piece of advice we are exposed to on a given day does not proceed from the Spirit of God. Some advice, in fact, is diametrically opposed to God's Spirit. Our culture, for example, may tell us to think only of ourselves, to amass as many material goods as we can, or to lie if it helps us to get ahead. The gift of discernment helps us to sort through these many messages in order to detect God's voice among the cacophony.

Good discernment is rooted in the conviction that we are loved by God. Anything that makes us doubt this fundamental truth is not from God. At the same time, discernment reminds us that we are sinners. This knowledge of our failings, rather than depressing us, only makes us more appreciative of God's mercy and more understanding of and compassionate toward others. Good discernment also calls us toward ever greater selflessness.

Good discernment is rooted in the conviction that we are loved by God.

It always asks, "Will this make me a more loving person?"

Discernment does not seek God's will in the abstract, wondering, "What is God's will for humankind?" Rather, it seeks God's will in the concrete, asking, "What is God's will for me in these particular circumstances?" Discernment, however, goes beyond wondering, "What does God want me to do here?" Ultimately it asks, "Who is God calling me to become?" In addition, discernment is not always individual. It can also be communal, asking, "Who is God calling us to become?"

In his book *Weeds Among the Wheat*, Thomas H. Green, SJ, says that good discernment presupposes several things: The first is that we have the desire to do God's will (Green calls this desire "a committed faith"). The second is that we have an openness to God's will (in other words, if we are wedded to our own will, discernment is impossible). The third is that discernment presupposes we have knowledge of God. If we don't know God personally through an ardent prayer life, how can we know what pleases God? For more serious discerning, it is often wise to seek the help of a good friend or spiritual director, someone who is familiar with the ways of God.

Green's final point is: "Discernment, like prayer, is an art. It is learned by doing, not just by reading about it."

How do I discern God's will in my own life? What factors help or hinder good discernment for me?

Spirit of Counsel, give me a discerning heart.

13 On Daring

The greatest hazard in life is to risk nothing.
—Leo F. Buscaglia

Jesus was a daring person. He dared to forsake the security and obscurity of an ordinary life in Nazareth and chose instead the life of an itinerant preacher, a life fraught with vulnerability and danger. When he started his preaching ministry and began to gain some notoriety, his relatives and hometown friends became embarrassed by his behavior. They tried to convince Jesus to forget this preaching life, to come back home, to settle down. When they saw he wasn't listening to reason, they tried force. But Jesus faced the challenge of their rationality and eluded their grasp.

Not only was Jesus himself daring, he dared others as well. When he was recruiting disciples, he did not pull any punches. He was ruthlessly honest with his followers, explaining in graphic detail what discipleship with him would entail. It would demand renunciation: "Foxes have dens and birds of the sky have nests, but the Son of Man has nowhere to rest his head" (Matthew 8:20). It would invite ridicule and persecution: "[They will] insult you and persecute you and utter every kind of evil against you" (Matthew 5:11). And it could even lead to death: "If these things are done when the wood is green, what will happen when it is dry?" (Luke 23:31).

Jesus never pretended that discipleship with him would be easy. He knew he was demanding of his followers a moral standard of living heretofore unseen. The disciples were shocked on a regular basis by many of the things Jesus said.

Being a Christian is tough. If we think otherwise, we are not living authentic Christianity. If we imagine, for example, that we are finally finished with forgiving, we are wrong. If we think we have shared more than enough with the poor, we are wrong. If we think we have successfully cleared the high bar of Christian love, then the bar is too low. Christianity is tough. In fact, left to our own resources, it is downright impossible. As Jesus himself told us, we can become his followers only through the generosity and power of the Holy Spirit.

Being a Christian is tough. If we think otherwise, we are not living authentic Christianity.

By offering daring as a gift of the Spirit, I am not saying that caution does not have a place in our lives. Of course it does. But I am suggesting that perhaps we allow caution too much sway in our decision-making—as individuals, parishes, local communities, and the Church. By saying things like "But we've never done that before" or "What will others think?" we cramp the Spirit's style and lessen the Spirit's effectiveness.

Once when I was on retreat, I found myself writing this short prayer in my journal, "God, help me to love you less cautiously." It is a prayer I still dare to say on a regular basis.

Do I find Christianity easy or tough? How daring am I when it comes to my faith?

Daring Spirit, help me this day to take some Christ-like risks.

14 On Desire

Jesus asked, "What are you looking for?"
—John 1:38

Many of us were taught to mistrust our desires. We were led to believe that all our desires were basically selfish or tainted. The whole concept of concupiscence was boiled down to this: "If you desire it, it must be bad. In fact, the more intensely you desire it, the worse it is!" We were told that happiness was found in denying our desires. In fact, we should really desire only one thing—to do God's will. We were seldom taught that we might discover God's will precisely by following our desires—to their deepest roots.

That's what Jesus taught about desires. One day, John the Baptist was preaching to the crowds when Jesus happened to walk by (John 1:35–42). Seeing Jesus, John pointed to him and said, "Behold, the Lamb of God." Some of John's disciples, hearing what he had said, began to follow Jesus. Jesus, aware that they were tailing him, turned around and asked them, "What are you looking for?" That question may very well be one of the most important questions in the Gospel. For what Jesus was really asking was, "What do you want?" or "What is it you desire?"

The disciples were caught off guard by Jesus' question. Flustered, they asked, "Master, where are you staying?" Jesus realized the inanity of their response, but he played right along and said, "Come and see." The disciples followed Jesus, saw where he was staying, and ended up spending the rest of the day with him. Their discipleship with Christ began by answering the question, "What are you looking for? What is it you desire?"

That was not the only occasion when Jesus led individuals to get in touch with their desires. To several sick people who approached him for a cure, Jesus asked, "What is it that you want?" or "What do you want me to do?" He never presumed to know what was inside another person's heart. He asked. By doing so, he helped people to discover and name their deepest desires for themselves.

A good way to begin praying is to ask ourselves the same question Jesus asked his first disciples: "What am I looking for?" That question can take a variety of forms: "What am I desiring right now?" "What would I like to see happen today?" "What do I want from this day?" "What do I desire for my life?" As we ask ourselves these questions, we must not be in too much of a hurry to answer them. Answering may take some time. In fact, we must even be ready to admit, "I don't know what I want." It can take a while to get down to the deepest desires of our heart. A quick response may be expressing only a surface desire: a new car, more money, peace and quiet, more time. But if we trace the root of these surface desires, we just might get in touch with some of our deeper longings: companionship, security, meaning, truth, love.

All our deepest desires will eventually lead to God. In other words, God is the fulfillment of all our longing.

I've saved the best news for last—all our deepest desires will eventually lead to God. In other words, God is the fulfillment of all our longing. What's more, God desires, too. God desires us! In fact, God desires us far more than we desire God. In that fact is our hope and salvation.

What am I looking for? If I really believed God desires me more than I desire God, what impact would that have on my life?

God of my longing, increase my desire for you.

15 On Discipline

The only authentic discipleship is a life of love lived unpretentiously for others out of a life lived for God.
—Brennan Manning

One day when I was about four, I crawled up onto the piano bench and began to fiddle with the keys. I was looking for "Jingle Bells." I knew it was in the keys—somewhere—because I had heard my mother and older sister playing it. I hit a key. Then another, and another. After much stopping and starting and stopping and starting, I finally found "Jingle Bells." The whole song! Heartened by my success, I began searching for other songs among the keys. Over time I found those, too: "Home on the Range," "It's Howdy Doody Time," and even "The Blue Skirt Waltz."

I thought I was ready to take piano lessons like my older sister, but I was told I had to wait until second grade. By the time I finally got that old, I was raring to go. With three years of playing by ear to my credit, I thought learning to play for real would be easy and fun. But I was wrong, and suddenly I was initiated into the harsh world of piano lessons.

First, I had to learn to read music. This meant staring for hours at flash cards, trying to distinguish between an F and an A, a G and an E. This seemed too much like work to me. In addition, I could no longer play just the songs I wanted to play. I now had to play the songs my piano teacher told me to play. And, quite frankly, I did not like some of those songs. And finally, I now had to practice. This meant I no longer played just when I felt like it, I had to play nearly every day—even when there were other things I preferred to do, like ride my bike or play with the cat.

My experience with piano lessons taught me a lot about discipline. It also taught me a lot about discipleship. The words *discipline* and *discipleship* are first cousins. To put it simply, it takes discipline to be a good disciple. What exactly is discipline? I see discipline as a channeling of energies. A good image of discipline for me has always been a rocket blasting off. The blast of any rocket is really a massive explosion—a massive channeled explosion. The energy of the blast is channeled to propel the rocket in a single direction, carrying it to its destination.

Being a disciple of Jesus is also all about the channeling of energy in a single direction—and the primary energy we channel is love. Discipline, then, is what enables us to live a life of love—which is precisely what discipleship means. Sometimes loving is easy. We can love when we want, whom we want, and on our own terms. But sooner or later, love will become more arduous. We will be called to love in ways we find difficult or nearly impossible. We will be asked to love some individuals we find unattractive, ornery, hurtful, or immoral. We will be invited to love on God's terms and not our own. And that is precisely what discipleship with Jesus means.

> *Being a disciple of Jesus is also all about the channeling of energy in a single direction—and the primary energy we channel is love.*

I ended up taking piano lessons for six years. To this day, I still like to sit down at a piano and plunk out not just "Jingle Bells," but things like "Moon River" and Tchaikovsky's "Piano Concerto No. 1." I never became a virtuoso, but I am very glad I had the discipline to stick with the lessons, because I still get a kick out of finding songs hidden in those keys.

What does discipline mean for me? How does my discipleship with Jesus channel my love?

Jesus, help me to live a life for others out of my love for you.

16 On Diversity

Diversity is not the enemy of unity. The enemy of unity is hatred or simply the lack of love.
—Demetrius Dumm, OSB

Many of us have a peculiar relationship with the concept of diversity. In one way we are all for it. "I wanna do my own thing! I have to express my individuality! I'm different from you and that's great!" But in another way, we mistrust it. "Diversity will destroy community! We have to do things alike! In unity is our strength!" We say we are all for diversity, yet we squelch any sign of it in ourselves and in others.

Why can we be so intolerant of diversity? For one thing, we may be afraid. Afraid of what? You name it! We are afraid of germs, wasps, snakes, lightning, strangers, heights, new ideas, the future, God, and even ourselves. These fears cause us to do some strange things—for example, to curb diversity. We reason that the more diversity there is, the less we will know and understand. The less we know and understand, the less control we will have over our life. And that's scary. That's bad.

We can curb diversity in small ways. We can demand that everyone act in the same way. We can say things like, "We should all dress alike." "We should all pray alike." "We should all hold the same values." People who are intolerant of diversity usually assume that there is really only one right way of doing things, one right way of being in the world. And it's their way (of course!).

But diversity is not a threat. It is a gift. In fact, it is one of the outstanding characteristics of God's creation. All we have to do is look at the world of plants and animals. When God thought "flower," God did not think merely daisy or rose. God thought lily, violet, geranium, orchid, hydrangea, daffodil, iris, jack-in-the-pulpit, pansy, aster, azalea, foxglove, lady's slipper, and so on.

St. Paul, in his first letter to the Corinthians, makes it clear that diversity is not only a characteristic of creation, it is also a characteristic of the Spirit. He writes: "There are different kinds of spiritual gifts but the same Spirit; there are different forms of service but the same Lord; there are different workings but the same God who produces all of them in everyone" (1 Corinthians 12:4–6). Paul sees the diversity among Christians as a reflection of the diversity among the Persons of the Blessed Trinity: the Spirit is the Holy Spirit, the Lord is Jesus, and God is the Father or Creator. Diversity, like all of God's creation, is essentially good.

Diversity, like all of God's creation, is essentially good.

What have been some of my experiences of diversity—especially in people? Do I see diversity as a blessing, a challenge, or both?

God of diversity, help me to appreciate and delight in what is different and unfamiliar.

17 On Failure

Mistakes are the usual bridge between inexperience and wisdom.
—Phyllis Theroux

We all know that it takes practice to do something well: from baking a lemon meringue pie, to playing a decent round of golf, to teaching third grade. We also know mistakes are inevitable when trying to master any skill or art. If we can accept such failures while learning to bake a soufflé or crochet an afghan, then why aren't we more accepting of the failures we make while learning to become a better person? Dare we even begin to see failure as a gift of the Spirit?

Dare we even begin to see failure as a gift of the Spirit?

Maybe we can if we view failure not as an end in itself, but as a stage in a process. When we fail, instead of crying, "I've failed!" and throwing up our hands in defeat, we could say, "I've failed here. Now what can I learn from this?" or "Where do I go from here?"

Years ago I read an article entitled "The Theology of Failure." The title stuck with me, for I believe that as Christians failure must be a part of our theology—or our theology is lacking. After all, Christianity is rooted in the cross. And what is the cross but one humongous failure? Sometimes we forget that. Maybe because we see too many pretty crosses—gold and silver ones, some with roses painted all over them. We forget that the cross was first and foremost an instrument of death and torture. Our wearing of a cross around our neck would be comparable to a French Revolutionary sporting a tiny guillotine, or a contemporary American wearing a replica of the electric chair.

We also forget that Christianity is rooted in failure because we know the final ending of Jesus' story. We know that it did not end with that cross; it ended with that empty tomb. But Jesus did not know that for sure when he sweated blood in Gethsemane. Certainly his followers did not know it when they laid his mutilated body in the tomb. As far as they were concerned, it was over. End of story.

That is what the two disciples on the road to Emmaus thought as they shuffled along, sharing their shock and disillusionment with each other (Luke 24:13–35). They also shared their disillusionment with a certain stranger who happened along and joined them on their way. "We had hoped . . . ," they said to him again and again. That stranger, of course, was Jesus. Gently and persistently, he opened the Scriptures to them with such force and clarity that their hearts began to burn within them. Finally, in an instant, they recognized him in the breaking of the bread. They realized that death is but a stepping-stone to eternal life, and failure a bridge to everlasting glory.

Have any of my mistakes and failures been a gift of the Spirit?

Jesus, help me to see my mistakes and failures as stepping-stones toward becoming a better person.

18 On Faith

Belief is a wise wager.
—Blaise Pascal

I remember the first time my father let me ride the tractor. I was probably about five. My father climbed up onto the tractor first, leaned over, and with one effortless motion of his giant arm, swooped me up into the seat with him. I felt very important—and a little afraid. The seat was higher than it looked from down below.

My father said, "Ready?" I nodded my head. "Good," he said. "Now you steer." Immediately I grabbed the steering wheel with both hands. He turned the key, the engine turned over, and the tractor shook beneath us. Over the roar of the motor, he said in my ear, "Now hang on," and he gently released the clutch. The tractor lurched forward. Instinctively I tightened my hands around the steering wheel. The tractor moved slowly at first, and then my father gave it more gas and we went a little faster, bouncing up and down together over the fields.

I wish I had a picture of my father and me on the tractor that first time. If I did, I know what I would see. Me with my back arched, arms stiff, hands clenching the steering wheel. On my face is a look of grim determination. After all, I am steering the tractor! Or at least I think I am. The photo would also show my father smiling, his one hand unobtrusively on the steering wheel, his other holding me gently but firmly in place. He is smiling because he knows the truth. He is in control of that tractor and he will see that no harm comes to me.

For me, riding the tractor with my father is a very good image of faith. Faith means being up high and moving forward. It means being eager, but maybe a little afraid, too. It means keeping your hands on the steering wheel and doing your part. But most importantly, faith means knowing whose hands are on the wheel with yours. It means knowing who is sitting with you and whose arms are cradling you. It means knowing that no real harm can come to you, no matter what.

Sometimes we use the wrong synonyms for faith; for example, we use the word *creed*. Kathleen Norris says in her book *Amazing Grace* that it is a mistake to reduce faith to dogmas. Faith is "not a list of 'things I believe,'" she writes, "but the continual process of learning (and relearning) what it means to love God, my neighbor, and myself." Faith, then, is not something I have, but rather it is someone I am becoming—a more loving person.

> *Faith, then, is not something I have, but rather it is someone I am becoming—a more loving person.*

For me, the best synonym for faith is trust. The word *trust* usually implies another person. That person, of course, is God, who is riding the tractor with us over the bumpy fields and steering us safely home.

What is my favorite image of faith? What helps me to trust in God?

God, give me a sense of your presence so I may better enjoy our ride together.

19 On Forgiveness

Forgiveness is having given up all hope of having a better past.
—Anne Lamott

On January 7, 1985 in Beirut, Lebanon, Father Lawrence Jenco, OSM, a program director for Catholic Relief Services, was kidnapped by Shiite Muslims. He was held hostage for 564 days. In his book *Bound to Forgive*, Jenco describes his time in captivity: the terror, the torture, the isolation. While reading it, one marvels how Jenco could survive such an ordeal. But one marvels even more at Jenco's ability to forgive his captors for all they had done to him.

In an interview shortly after the book came out (*U.S. Catholic*, March 1996), a reporter asked Jenco how long it took him to start forgiving his captors. Jenco replied: "From day one." He went on to explain, "When you read the Scriptures, God's words of forgiveness appear throughout . . . If you don't forgive, you end up with a tremendous amount of hate and resentment." In fact, when he thought he was going to die in captivity, Jenco wanted to do so with the words of Jesus on his lips, "Father, forgive them for they know not what they do."

Although Jenco forgave his captors, he did not forget what they had done to him. "People say, 'Oh, forgive and forget' as if it's a mandate from God," he said. "But it doesn't work that way. I have all kinds of memories, and when I recall, I heal." When asked if he would tell others they ought to forgive, Jenco replied, "You must ask God for that gift. We are constantly going to God to ask for forgiveness, so why don't we ask God for the generosity to forgive as God forgives?"

Not many of us will end up being hostages like Jenco. Yet we can learn much about forgiveness from his experience. "The essence of my faith commitment is love," said the priest. "And the core of that is forgiveness." When Jenco shared his experience with people, some of them wept. Jenco believed they were not really crying for him, but rather because he had touched their own pain and suffering, and even sometimes their own lack of forgiveness.

The reason we forgive is simple. As Father Jenco said, "[forgiveness is] the cost of being a follower of Jesus."

And so, we learn to forgive—to forgive ourselves, to forgive others. We forgive the driver who cuts in front of us in traffic and the spouse who embarrasses us at the party. We forgive our church, our nation, our human race. The reason we forgive is simple. As Father Jenco said, "[forgiveness is] the cost of being a follower of Jesus. You have to make Jesus' message a part of your life. You have to be the sacrament to the world of Jesus' love."

Am I a forgiving person? Have I ever experienced the forgiveness of another?

Jesus, forgiving one, please help me to be the sacrament of your forgiveness in my own little part of the world.

20 On Fortitude

With God, nothing, not even a headache, is lost.
—Blessed Lydwina of Schiedam

Several years ago the French painter André Girard was attending the opening of a chapel he had decorated. A woman approached him and said, "Mr. Girard, I do not like your crucifixion. It is so unpleasant." "Madame," Girard replied, "it was an unpleasant occasion."

As Christians, we are sometimes uncomfortable with unpleasantness. We prefer, for example, to dwell on the nice things Jesus said: "You are worth more than many sparrows" (Matthew 10:31). "Do not be afraid, little flock" (Luke 12:32). "Peace be with you" (John 20:19). We sometimes gloss over the other things Jesus said that aren't quite so pleasant: "Whoever wishes to come after me must deny himself, take up his cross, and follow me" (Matthew 16:24). "Behold I am sending you like sheep in the midst of wolves" (Matthew 10:16). "I have come to set a man against his father, a daughter against her mother" (Matthew 10:35).

Unpleasantness, of course, is a fact of life. We find it even in Jesus' nicest parables. Before the Good Samaritan came along and ministered so lovingly to the man lying on the side of the road, a group of hoodlums first robbed the man, beat him to a pulp, and left him for dead. Before the prodigal son was welcomed back into his father's outstretched arms, he insult his father, squandered a fortune on loose living, and wallowed in the mud with pigs. Although poor, sore-covered Lazarus was eventually relieved of his misery and given an eternal reward, the rich man who was blind to Lazarus' suffering was punished for his lack of compassion.

Sometimes we even downplay the crucifixion. After Vatican II, there was a movement to remove Jesus' body altogether from the cross or to replace the twisted, dead corpus with a triumphantly risen one.

Yes, Jesus is risen. Yes, he will never die again. Yes, our faith is anchored in the reality of that empty tomb. But the fact remains that Jesus was raised only after he had passed through the crucifixion. And we will be raised with Jesus only after we have passed through unpleasantness of our own. Walter Burghardt, SJ, reminds us of this when he says: "a spirituality not intimately nailed to Calvary is a Christian mirage."

The gift of the Holy Spirit that keeps our spirituality nailed to Calvary is called fortitude. It is the gift that enables us to endure and/or work through pain and suffering. In his book *For You Departed*, South African writer Alan Paton tells the poignant story of the death of his wife, a death characterized by prolonged suffering. Throughout the book, Paton addresses his deceased wife directly. At one point he writes, "Where did your courage come from? It was your religion, of course, that strange Christianity of yours that took seriously the story of the cross, that understood with perfect clarity that one might have to suffer for doing what was right, that rejected absolutely that kind of cross-less geniality that calls itself Christianity."

> *The gift of the Holy Spirit that keeps our spirituality nailed to Calvary is called fortitude.*

Our model of fortitude is Jesus on the cross. When we reflect on the crucifixion, it is important to look beneath the sufferings Jesus endured and see the love that made his endurance possible. Anthony Padovano says, "Christ does not suffer because suffering is in itself a value, but because love without restraint requires suffering. It is not a love for suffering which Christ reveals, but a love which prevails in suffering."

The love that prevails in suffering is another name for fortitude.

What are some of the crosses I am bearing right now? How is my faith helping me to endure and/or work through these sufferings?

Spirit, give me the gift of fortitude, that my love may prevail in everything I do or endure.

21 On Gentleness

You can no more win a war than you can win an earthquake.
—Jeannette Rankin

We live in a world of violence. Every day the news media run stories of women being murdered by their boyfriends, teenagers overdosing on drugs, bombs exploding in marketplaces, young girls being raped on their way to school, store clerks being shot in robberies, criminals being executed by the state, war planes bombing rebel forces. Then there is the violence that goes largely unreported, but is just as real: spouses screaming profanities at each other, teachers humiliating students in front of others, women opting for abortions, neighbors spreading gossip about neighbors, parents swatting kids on the head, kids punching other kids on the playground, women bashing men and men bashing women.

Into this mess steps Jesus, who says, "Learn of me, for I am gentle and humble of heart" (Matthew 11:29). And we want to say, "Are you kidding? Gentle? Humble? In this day and age?" And Jesus is likely to reply, "Yes, in this day and age, more than ever."

What exactly is the gift of gentleness? Gentleness is a welcoming disposition toward life—all of life. That includes God (of course), others, me, and the whole of creation. Although we do not hear much about gentleness these days, it certainly is mentioned a lot in Scripture—especially in the New Testament. Jesus counseled gentleness by both word and action. One of his Beatitudes was about gentleness: "Blessed are the meek" (Matthew 5:5). Meekness is another word for gentleness. Jesus told his followers to turn the other cheek when they were struck rather than retaliate (Luke 6:29). When

> *Gentleness is a welcoming disposition toward life—all of life.*

his apostles wanted to call down fire on the Samaritan village that refused to receive him, Jesus rebuked them for even considering such a violent thing (Luke 9:51–55). And when his enemies came to arrest him in the garden (John 18:1–13), and Peter clumsily tried to defend him by chopping off the ear of the high priest's slave, Jesus ordered, "Put your sword back into its sheath—for Pete's sake!" (I added that last part. It seemed to fit.) Jesus was gentle all the way to his unjust execution on the cross, thus giving us an incredible ideal to strive for—to be gentle and nonviolent even amid persecution.

How do we even begin to measure up to such an ideal of gentleness? We begin by acknowledging that we have the capacity to be very "ungentle"—that is, to hurt, maim, or even kill. All of us do. No exceptions.

We can also become gentler by becoming more aware of the little ways we do violent things. Thomas Merton once said that when he undertook to become nonviolent, he started by closing doors softly. Perhaps we can start there too. Then we can move on to other things, such as walking more slowly, speaking more respectfully to people— especially those who share the same house with us—using gender inclusive language, letting someone else go ahead of us in the check-out line, driving less frantically, eating foods that are healthy for us, visiting an elderly friend, volunteering at a shelter for abused women, getting more involved in promoting justice, and praying for peace in our hearts and in the world.

Gentleness is not weakness. It is strength. It is not cowardliness. It is courage. But it is also somewhat unnatural. The natural response to life's pricks or stabs is to lash out in violence. As followers of Jesus, however, we embrace another way, the way of gentleness. It is a gentleness rooted in the trust of a God who loves us more than we can begin to imagine.

How gentle am I toward others and myself? Have I ever turned the other cheek?

Gentle Jesus, give me a gentle heart even amid persecution.

22 On Guilt

Each snowflake in an avalanche pleads not guilty.
—Stanislaw Lem

We live in an age that belittles guilt. Whenever we talk about guilt—whether it's Catholic guilt, Irish guilt, feminine guilt, or just plain guilty guilt—we usually do so in a pejorative way. Our culture tells us that guilt is bad. Or worse, "You shouldn't feel guilty about anything." Even when we do some apparently bad things—spit at people, cheat on a test, steal a car, or even kill someone—we don't have to feel guilty. We can always blame something or someone else for our bad behavior: "The devil made me do it." "My rotten childhood made me do it." "My genes made me do it." "Society made me do it." In a nation of victims, guilt is a rare commodity.

That's too bad, because guilt, properly understood, is a gift of the Spirit. It is one of the ways the Spirit directs our decision making. Guilt can encourage us to do the right thing, to make choices that are life-giving, and to feel sorry when our choices don't measure up to our dignity as children of God. Guilt, in this healthy sense, is largely an acceptance of responsibility for wrongdoing. When we scream at our spouse because of something that happened at work, for example, we should feel guilty. When we never have time for our loved ones, we should feel guilty. When we cling selfishly to our time and resources, we should feel guilty. When 1.5 billion people in this world are impoverished

Guilt can encourage us to do the right thing, to make choices that are life-giving, and to feel sorry when our choices don't measure up to our dignity as children of God.

beyond any shred of human dignity, and we have more than we need, we should feel guilty.

But guilt can be twisted into a form that is spiritually unhealthy or even lethal. This happens when, instead of urging us to run into the arms of our forgiving God, guilt paralyzes us. It makes us focus on our sins and forget about repentance or conversion. (In some ways, that's easier!) Guilt is bad if we wallow in it. This happens when we constantly stand before God (or curl up in the fetal position before God), beat our breasts, and cry out how wretched we are. We may be wretched—more or less—but there is nothing life-giving about wallowing in wretchedness. As Father Joseph Creedon says so well: "All of us are sinners: big deal. All of us are forgiven by God: now that is a big deal."

It is fascinating to note, when reading the lives of the saints, how many of them saw themselves as grave sinners. They seemed very comfortable with acknowledging their guilt and sin not only before God, but before the whole world. But notice, they didn't stop with their sin. They always went on to speak of God's great love. A saint in point is St. Paul. Paul saw himself as a great sinner. He had good reason, too. After all, didn't he participate in rounding up Christians for food for hungry lions? Didn't he participate in the stoning of St. Stephen? Talk about guilt! But Paul never described himself as a sinner without, at the same time, referring to God's grace—which not only forgave him, but enabled him to be a useful instrument in the furthering of God's Kingdom. Without minimizing his sins, Paul refused to be paralyzed by them. As such, he is a fine example of what a healthy sense of guilt can do for all of us.

Have I ever experienced guilt as the first step toward repentance and conversion? Have I ever wallowed in guilt?

God, I have sinned. May my sense of guilt lead me to make life-giving choices.

23 On Healing

You are the salve that purifies our souls; you are the ointment that
heals our wounds.
—Hildegard of Bingen

The four evangelists are unanimous on this point—Jesus was a healer.
In Mark's Gospel, for instance, Jesus bursts onto the public scene
amid a flurry of healing activity. The other three evangelists paint a
similar picture of Jesus. In fact, Matthew places this summary at the
beginning of Jesus' ministry: "He went around all of Galilee, teaching
in their synagogues, proclaiming the gospel of the kingdom, and curing every disease and illness among the people" (Matthew 4:23).

The truth is, however, Jesus did not cure every disease and illness.
In fact, if we read the Gospels carefully, we will see that, despite all the
cures he wrought, Jesus was something of a reluctant healer. In fact,
Jesus seldom took the initiative in curing others; the sick had to come
to him and specifically ask for a cure. Only on rare occasions—for
example, the cure of the son of the widow of Naim—did Jesus himself
initiate the healing.

Why this reluctance to heal people? For one thing, Jesus knew
there was something far more important than physical healings.
Namely, faith. In fact, most of Jesus' cures were a direct response to
someone's faith. Jesus emphasized this link between healing and faith
on numerous occasions.

Ultimately, though, Jesus came among us to heal not bodies, but
souls. After all, every person Jesus healed during his ministry eventually died. The point of the cures was not to extend earthly life forever.
The point was to restore eternal life now—and the cures were but a
sign of that restoration. Jesus, therefore, was far more interested in

restoring spiritual sight than physical sight. He was more concerned with cleansing from sin than from leprosy. His basic call was not, "Be healed!" It was, "Repent!" The Cistercian monk Thomas Keating sees a connection between repentance and healing. In fact, he calls repentance "that fundamental call in the Gospel to begin the healing process."

This gift of the Holy Spirit reminds us that we are all ill no matter how healthy we may be physically. We all suffer from maladies of the soul. What are some of those spiritual maladies? We may be crippled by guilt, paralyzed by fear, blind to the truth, deaf to the cry of the poor. Or we may be imprisoned by addictive behaviors, bent over from despair, or living with a broken heart. The healing process begins when we repent—that is, turn to Jesus and hear him ask us, as he asked so many sick people in the Gospels, "What would you like me to do for you?"

The healing process begins when we repent—that is, turn to Jesus and hear him ask us, as he asked so many sick people in the Gospels, "What would you like me to do for you?"

And may we simply say to him, "Heal me. Heal me. Heal me." And may we do whatever Jesus tells us to do to begin the healing process.

What are some of my spiritual maladies? Do I really believe Jesus can heal me?

Healing Jesus, make me whole.

24 On Initiative

If you just sit around and wait, the only thing that happens is you get older.

—Anonymous

Initiative means to start something, to take the first step. It means to not sit around on your butt waiting for someone else to do something, but to get up off the couch and do it yourself. Jesus appreciated initiative. He seemed pleased, for example, that a few of the disciples came to him on their own initiative (John 1:35–42), thus saving him the trouble of seeking them out. Jesus also seemed to enjoy the persevering initiative of the Canaanite woman who refused to take no for an answer, but kept bugging Jesus until she nearly drove the apostles crazy (Matthew 15:21–28). And Jesus must have laughed when he saw the heights to which Zacchaeus's initiative carried him—to the top of that sycamore tree. Jesus rewarded Zacchaeus's initiative, too, by calling him down and dining in his house—much to the shock of the self-righteous and more passive onlookers (Luke 19:1–10).

Jesus not only appreciated initiative when he saw it, he encouraged it when he didn't see it. He once told his disciples to be simple as doves, yes, but clever as serpents. Cleverness presupposes a certain amount of initiative, don't you think? Besides, have you ever met a cobra that was a doormat? Jesus also told a parable about a steward with an incredible amount of initiative. Rather than wait around for his master to fire him because of some crooked things he had done, the steward cleverly arranged things to insure himself a warm welcome from others when he was thrown out into the street. Now that was initiative!

Jesus encouraged initiative in his disciples mainly by calling them to action. He didn't say, "Now you guys just sit around here and wait until the people come to you." No, he sent them out—all seventy-two of them—to go where the people were and to preach the good news—proactively.

But the biggest news that Jesus proclaimed about initiative was that God is the Great Initiator. God is the great Starter-of-Everything. After all, it was God who literally began everything with the first "Let there be light!"

The gift of initiative reminds us that, as Christians, we are called to action. We are called to start things. We are called not merely to respond to life's events, but to play an active role in determining their course. By doing so, we will become more and more like our God, the Initiator of All.

We are called not merely to respond to life's events, but to play an active role in determining their course.

Have I taken any initiative lately to spread the Good News? Do I play an active role in determining the course of my life?

Initiating Spirit, help me to start something good today.

25 On Instinct

A good person is not one who does the right thing, but one who is in the habit of doing the right thing.
—Abraham Heschel

When we hear the word *instinct*, many of us immediately think, "Instinct is something animals have to insure their survival and propagation." But humans also have instincts. I learned in biology class years ago that infants are born with two instincts—to suck and to cry. Infants begin to suck while they are still in the womb, gearing up their little mouths for their first taste of milk. Then there is the other instinct—crying. Crying is the instinct a baby has to communicate that something is wrong and, thus, better assure its survival.

Because we tend to identify instinct with animals, we often equate it with our so-called "animal nature." Sex is an instinct, we say. So is the drive to get ahead, to accumulate wealth, to bully others. The story of the Fall in Genesis reinforces our conception that instinct is bad. Because of the sin of our first parents, some say that we all are essentially corrupt. But the doctrine of the total corruption of humankind is hard to reconcile with experience. When I was sixteen years old, for instance, I met a boy my age who, two years earlier, had rushed into a burning house to rescue two small boys who had been playing with matches. Considerable attention was given to his act of heroism, including the awarding of a medal. But the boy confided to me that he felt uncomfortable with all the fuss. "At the time, I never even thought of the danger to myself," he said. "I just thought of getting those kids out!" Wasn't that instinct?

We are made in the image and likeness of God. Then surely that means some of our instincts are godlike. Some are. The trick, of course, is being able to identify those instincts that are godlike and those that are not. Jesus gave us a litmus test to discern the difference. His words about distinguishing between true and false prophets can also help us to distinguish between good and bad instincts: "By their fruits you will know them" (Matthew 7:16). We can ask ourselves: "If I follow this instinct, what will it do to me, my relationships, my goals, and my level of happiness?" "Does following this instinct bring peace, self-esteem, a sense of harmony, joy?"

The truth is, good instincts have their origin in God. Maybe good instincts are simply another name for grace.

As Christians, we need friends, spiritual friends, who can give us feedback on the choices we are making, the instincts we are following. The fact remains that our instincts, no matter how noble they seem or how well they have served us in the past, could still lead us astray. The truth is, good instincts have their origin in God. Maybe good instincts are simply another name for grace.

What are some of my good instincts? Who are some of my spiritual friends who help guide me?

Gracious God, help me to follow those instincts of mine that have their origin in you.

26 On Intimacy

True knowledge leads to love.
—William Wordsworth

What, exactly, is intimacy? First of all, it is not the same as having sex. Two people can have a deep, intimate relationship without ever engaging in sex. Conversely, two people can have sex and not have an intimate relationship.

Second, intimacy involves a relationship between two persons. Both words are important. *Two*—I cannot be intimate by myself. *Persons*—I can't truly be intimate except with another person. Yes, I can have an affectionate relationship with my dog or parakeet or even my car, but intimacy presupposes a deeper kind of sharing that can exist only between two persons.

Third, intimacy involves a mutual sharing between those persons. If only one person shares, that is not intimacy. Intimacy presupposes that I allow myself to be known by another, and that I allow the other person to make himself or herself known to me. It is a relationship of mutual respect in which both parties can be who they are.

And finally, intimacy takes time. Strictly speaking, we cannot have an intimate relationship with someone we have known for only five minutes or even five days. The depth of sharing involved in intimacy presupposes a significant length of association.

With regard to intimacy, the good news of the Bible is this: God desires intimacy with us. God called Abraham not only to a new homeland, but also to a deep, personal relationship with him. This relationship is characterized by honesty, mutual give-and-take, and trust. Scripture is replete with other individuals who were on intimate terms with God: Jacob, Moses, Joseph, Gideon, Judith, Ruth,

David, Joseph, Mary. Their lives demonstrated that God wishes to know us and to be known by us.

The clearest evidence of God's desire for intimacy with us is the person of Jesus.

The clearest evidence of God's desire for intimacy with us is the person of Jesus. In fact, we can say that Jesus' coming into our world proves just how much God wants to know us and be known by us. Jesus was on intimate terms with God, going so far as to call God "Abba." He was on intimate terms with his disciples, saying to them at the Last Supper, "I call you friends" (John 15:15). He encouraged intimacy among his followers, calling them to mutual love and forgiveness, intimacy's two greatest tools.

Today we might want to ask ourselves, with whom do I have an intimate relationship? How do I nurture intimacy with others? Have I ever experienced God's desire to be intimate with me? How do I share myself with God and allow God to share him/herself with me?

In what ways has intimacy been a gift for me personally? What have been some of the challenges of intimacy?

God, I thank you for the gift of intimacy. Let me experience today your desire to know me and to be known by me.

27 On Kindness

*When I was young, I admired clever people. Now that I am old,
I admire kind people.*
—Abraham Heschel

Why is kindness so difficult? For one thing, it demands that I act in a selfless way to these human beings right in front of me: this coworker who cracks her gum all day, this elderly woman who talks incessantly, this teenage boy who is such a smart aleck, this next door neighbor who plays his music too loud.

Love, in contrast, can be more distant. Because Jesus calls us to love everybody, we can say, "I love the people in Sri Lanka," and probably mean it. But ordinarily, we cannot say we are kind to the people in Sri Lanka unless we are in Sri Lanka. It is far easier to love people who live half a world away than it is to be kind to the person who lives next door.

It is far easier to love people who live half a world away than it is to be kind to the person who lives next door.

Kindness is also difficult because it is so concrete. It almost always makes some specific, personal demand upon us. Kindness says, "Help carry those groceries—now! Offer to change that tire—now! Run to the store for milk—now!" Kindness is usually obvious, too. There's almost no mistaking kindness when you see it—or mistaking its absence when you do not. Love, on the other hand, is not always that concrete or obvious. We can say we love our children, for example, even when we are disciplining them—and we are loving them! Love can be faked more easily than kindness. But faked kindness is easy to spot. It even has a name: obsequiousness.

Kindness is difficult for yet another reason. In his article entitled "Kindness" (*America*, Feb. 14, 1998), Father William O'Malley, SJ, says that kindness goes beyond the Golden Rule. He writes, "'Do unto others as you would have others do unto you' is not the touchstone of any one religion; it is a matter of human survival. . . . But kindness takes one step further, beyond morality, into unreflective loving."

Unreflective loving. That is a good definition of kindness. But how do we learn to be kind? How do we come to love unreflectively? We probably begin by seeing the kindness of others. When I was growing up on our small farm in Ohio, for example, I was being instructed in the ways of kindness without even knowing it. My mother used to bake quite regularly. Two of her specialties were apple pies and rye bread. On many occasions I can remember her saying, "Take the Stevensons this loaf of bread," or "Take this apple pie to Shinky" (the hired hand who lived on the farm next door). When road workers were fixing our road under the hot summer sun, my mother sent us kids out with a pitcher of water or lemonade for them. Similarly, my father, who always had a big garden, was forever giving things away—beans, tomatoes, strawberries, corn. The example of my parents' many acts of kindness, of unreflective loving, made a lasting impression on me.

Jesus calls us to love everybody. He also calls us to be kind to the individuals we meet each day. It can be particularly challenging to be kind to the people we live with. Because we see them so often, we tend to take them for granted—like the tile on the kitchen floor or the picture on the living room wall. It is easy to drift into the habit of speaking curtly to the ones we live with, ignoring them, or being downright rude to them. Remember, Kindness, like her big sister Charity, always begins at home. In his famous "Hymn to Charity" (1 Corinthians 13:1–13), St. Paul wisely says that love, if it is genuine, is kind.

How did I first learn about kindness? How kind am I now?

Loving God, teach me to be kind.

28 On Leadership

*If I, therefore, the master and teacher, have washed your feet, you
ought to wash one another's feet.*
—Jesus (John 13:14)

One of the great leaders of the Church in our day was Joseph Cardinal
Bernardin of Chicago. As Bernardin lay in a hospital recuperating
from cancer surgery, his friend Eugene Kennedy delivered an eloquent
testimony to him at the annual meeting of the U.S. bishops. What
Kennedy said about Bernardin can be applied
to any good leader: "[He] has never been afraid
of the dark and, in his company, neither are
we." People like Cardinal Bernardin teach us a
lot about leadership. I would like to share seven
lessons I have learned about the gift of leadership from people such as Bernardin.

> "[He] has never
> been afraid of
> the dark and,
> in his company,
> neither are we."

1. Leadership is the capacity to influence others for the better. Good
   leadership is always directed toward liberation.
2. There are various forms of leadership: charismatic, administrative,
   and executive are just a few. Each type has both positive and negative aspects. The type that is best for a particular group will vary
   according to time, place, and circumstances.
3. Exercising leadership is not the same as exercising authority. As
   Richard McCormick, SJ, has said, "One can command all day
   without being a leader for a minute."
4. We can be leaders without wearing badges, carrying crosiers,
   banging gavels, or sitting behind big desks. Parents and teachers,
   for example, are leaders.

5. At the Last Supper, Jesus gave his apostles a memorable picture of the type of leadership he was calling for. Wrapping a towel around his waist and kneeling down, he began to wash the feet of his disciples. Leadership for Jesus was never about privilege; it was always about service.

6. The poet William Butler Yeats wrote, "The real leader serves truth, not people." In other words, good leaders resist the temptation to merely please people.

7. Good leaders do not make tensions go away. James Bacik, a theologian and diocesan priest, says that what we need is a "dialectical spirituality"—that is, spirituality that understands the tensions of our age and allows us to bring forth good fruit. What tensions? The tension between the individual and community, the traditional and the new, the eternal and the ever changing.

Who for me has been a model of servant leadership? What are some of the ways I exercise leadership in my life?

Jesus, help me to believe in leadership as compassionate service.

29 On Learning

Each step is the place to learn.
—Sue Bender

When I reflect on the gift of learning, I came up with the following
observations:

Learners are humble. They know how much they don't know.
Once I lived with a sister with whom everyone was having a hard
time. Another sister said to me, "The problem with her is she thinks
she knows everything." I had to agree. Learners are easier to live with
than non-learners. They have more friends, too.

Learners also have more fun. That is because they are curious.
When they do not know something, they do not say, "I don't know"
and go back to lying on the couch. They say, "I don't know, but I'd like
to find out," and they reach for an encyclopedia, click on the Internet,
or run to the phone and call a friend who might know. Learners are seldom bored because they are always learning something new. Learners
are seldom boring, either. They are interesting people because they are
interested people.

Genuine learners can learn under any circumstances. They never
wait for ideal conditions. If they are caught in a traffic jam, or their
flight was canceled, or they are about to undergo toe surgery, they
are learning something. All experiences—positive, negative, or somewhere in between—can teach them something new about themselves
and about life. Learners tend to be flexible. They have to be, for every
time they learn something new, they are changed by it. It is as if every
new piece of information or insight or experience causes a new groove
or wrinkle in their brain (or heart!).

Learners know the most effective way to learn something is through experience. They know that there is a big difference between being told the bread is delicious and actually cutting a slice, smearing it with butter, and eating it. At the same time, learners are very good at learning from the experience of others. They tend to be good listeners, good observers, and good readers.

Learners know the most effective way to learn something is through experience.

Jesus liked learners. We learn this from the Gospels. His favorite people were individuals who were humble, curious, flexible, interesting, and open to change. One of Jesus' favorite words was *learn*. He frequently invited his listeners to learn from his teachings and parables. His main invitation to the people he spoke to was simply this: "Learn from me" (Matthew 11:29).

To what extent am I a learner? What have I learned recently from my own experience or the experience of others?

God of truth, may all my learning and yearning lead me to you today.

30 On Levity

Those who believe in Christ will laugh unhesitatingly in everlasting glory.
—St. Pionius

Marc Gellman is a rabbi on Long Island. Tom Hartman is a priest, also on Long Island. Several years ago they were both invited by a local cable TV station in New York to discuss the similarities between Passover and Easter. Says Hartman, "Right away, we hit it off. It was magic." Gellman agrees and adds, "Both Tom and I realized religion had not been covered well, or at all, by the media." The two men decided to do something about that. They offered to be the religion guys for a major TV network. Within a short time, they were appearing regularly on both TV and radio, discussing everything from prayer to suffering, from morals to death.

But it is not just the fact that a rabbi and a priest are discussing religion together that is noteworthy. It is how they are discussing religion together—with wit and humor. Gellman explains, "One reason religion is not being listened to is that it takes itself so seriously. It's sometimes presented in such a humorless, accusatory, and guilt-provoking way that people's reaction is, 'I don't want any more of this.' It's sort of like castor oil."

Both men are convinced that God wants us to laugh. When asked what the best proof is that God has a sense of humor, Gellman replies, "The platypus. A god who could make an animal like that is definitely funny." Hartman adds, "And look around at the way God made people. You gotta laugh. People are very funny."

Father Hartman and Rabbi Gellman are doing everyone a big service by introducing levity into their discussions of religion. Religion and levity should go together. In fact, levity is one of the gifts of the Holy Spirit. Elton Trueblood, a Protestant minister, would agree. He warned, "Never trust a theologian who doesn't have a sense of humor."

Similarly, Friedrich Nietzsche, a nineteenth-century German philosopher, once had a vision of Satan. Nietzsche described the devil as "the spirit of gravity."

In a world that constantly bombards us with bad news, levity is not easy to sustain. But levity is not blind to this bad news. On the contrary, it sees clearly the injustice and suffering around and within us. But levity believes that injustice and suffering, in light of God's promises, are never ultimate. Or, to put it another way, levity sees further than gravity. It sees deeper. It sees more. Dr. John McBride, a psychotherapist, summed it up well when he said, "The ability to laugh at ourselves is the next greatest gift we have to love."

> "The ability to laugh at ourselves is the next greatest gift we have to love."

How much levity is there in my life? What helps me not to take myself so seriously?

God of levity and laughter, help me to lighten up.

31 On Liberation

Freedom is nothing else but the chance to be better.
—Albert Camus

As I stood in St. Wenceslaus Square in the heart of Prague a few years back, several images came to my mind. I recalled photographs of the uprising against the Communists in 1968. I remembered one picture in particular. It showed a young student waving a sign with my last name on it—*Svoboda*, which means, "freedom." Unfortunately, those cries for liberty in 1968 were answered with arrests, bullets, and tanks. The next images that came to my mind were TV news clips of the revolution of 1989. This massive and largely peaceful uprising, unlike the one in 1968, proved successful, and the Czech people won their freedom (their "svoboda") from Communist oppression. Later, as I listened to my relatives tell stories of what it was like to live under Communist rule for forty years, I thought, "Only those who have been enslaved can begin to appreciate liberation."

"Only those who have been enslaved can begin to appreciate liberation."

Liberation is one of the major themes in the Bible. In the Old Testament, the Greek word for liberation is *eleutheroo*, which literally means "to be snatched from slavery." The Old Testament speaks of two great liberations: the freeing of Israel from the slavery of Egypt and later from the slavery of Babylon. Both liberations were viewed as the direct result of the goodness and power of God.

When Jesus came onto the scene, he spoke of his mission in terms of liberation. Standing up in his hometown synagogue one Sabbath, he read a passage from the prophet Isaiah and identified himself with these words: "The Spirit of the Lord is upon me. . . . He has sent me to proclaim liberty to captives" (Luke 4:18). Some of Jesus' listeners assumed he was speaking of political liberation—that is, the freeing of the Jews from Roman domination. It was a misunderstanding that plagued Jesus' ministry all the way to Calvary.

St. Paul, who knew a lot about liberation, claimed that Jesus also freed us from the law: "Sin is not to have any power over you, since you are not under the law but under grace" (Romans 6:14). This doesn't mean we ignore all law. Rather, it means we no longer look exclusively to exterior law for our principle of salvation. Instead, our new norm of conduct becomes docility to the Spirit, poured out into our hearts. Paul still speaks of the law of Christ on occasion, but this is the new law, summed up best in the word *love*.

One final note: I called this gift of the Spirit not *freedom* but *liberation*. I did this on purpose. Freedom sounds too much like a done deal to me, whereas liberation implies a process. And that's an important difference. For as it was once said, "Liberty is always unfinished business."

To what extent have I attained liberation? What gets in the way of my being free?

God, thank you for making me your child. Jesus, thank you for freeing me from sin. Spirit, thank you for liberating me from selfishness.

32 On Lowliness

Big doesn't necessarily mean better. Sunflowers aren't better than violets.
—Edna Ferber

Throughout his ministry, Jesus makes a big deal out of smallness. He primarily chose as his disciples ordinary and insignificant individuals. Although he preaches his message to all, he directs it especially to those who are poor and lowly. Later, he compares the Kingdom of God to a tiny mustard seed. Jesus tells his followers that if they wish to become his disciples, they must become as little children, they must strive to be the least. Finally, he says of himself, "I am meek and humble of heart" (Matthew 11:29).

Smallness. Lowliness. Meekness. Not exactly the watchwords of our day. On the contrary, ours is a world where bigger is better, where we overuse the prefixes *mega*, *super*, and *ultra*. Ours is a culture that glorifies power and rewards audacity. Perhaps more than ever, then, we need the gift of the Spirit that enables us to respect smallness, celebrate lowliness, and befriend meekness.

The gift of lowliness helps us to appreciate smallness in all its forms: youth, inexperience, ordinariness, illness, poverty, power-lessness, incompleteness, inadequacy, prebirth, old age. Today, we might want to take a reality check of our attitude toward least-ness. For example, how do I respond to children? Am I protective of their lives, attentive to their needs, concerned for their future? What about the elderly? Am I appreciative of their past accomplishments, patient with their infirmities, mindful of their well-being? How do I respond to the lowly whom I encounter in everyday life—the poor, the sick, the physically and mentally challenged, the ignorant, the imprisoned, the sinner?

How do I respond when I experience smallness and lowliness within myself? Am I content to be ordinary? Am I patient with my sins and failures? Do I acknowledge my shortcomings, my incompleteness? When I experience my powerlessness, what do I do? Throw up my hands in despair or reach out for the ever-ready hand of God?

St. Paul not only accepted his lowliness, he boasted about it. To the Corinthians, he wrote these magnificent words: "If I must boast, I will boast of the things that show my weakness" (2 Corinthians 11:30). Why? Because Paul heard and believed these words Jesus spoke to him: "My grace is sufficient for you, for power is made perfect in weakness" (2 Corinthians 12:9). May we, like Paul, be able to proclaim, "For when I am weak, then I am strong" (2 Corinthians 12:10).

> *How do I respond when I experience smallness and lowliness within myself? Am I content to be ordinary?*

What is my attitude toward smallness and lowliness? Do I really believe that God loves the lowly?

God of the lowly, fill my weakness with your saving power.

33 On Mercy

God is mercy within mercy within mercy.
—Thomas Merton

The spiritual works of mercy are a venerable tradition in the Church. There are seven of them. Let's take a quick look at each one.

1. *Admonish the sinner.* This work of mercy is rooted in the belief that sin leads us away from God and others. It separates us from love and eventually ends in misery. Sometimes this work of mercy means telling people what they may not want to hear. Most often it means living our faith in such a way that others find it immensely attractive.
2. *Instruct the ignorant.* Good instruction helps people to see things in a new perspective. It has the power to change attitudes and transform behavior. Parents perform this work of mercy every time they teach their children how to be better people.
3. *Counsel the doubtful.* Doubt can assume many forms, but perhaps the most prevalent is doubt about one's self-worth. We can help alleviate this doubt in others by addressing them respectfully, listening to them, complimenting them, doing small favors for them, offering encouraging words, asking them for help, thanking them, and spending time with them.
4. *Comfort the sorrowful.* Comforting the sorrowful is seldom easy. We tend to feel helpless, awkward, at a loss for words. It is good to remember that most of the time the sorrowful do not need a lot of words; they need only a little of our compassionate presence.
5. *Bear wrongs patiently.* Jesus told us, "Take up your cross and follow me" (Matthew 16:24). He didn't say, "If you have a cross,

take it up." No, he assumed we would have one. This work of mercy reminds us that crosses, or wrongs, are inevitable in life. We should not be surprised or feel guilty, therefore, when we experience them.

6. *Forgive all injuries.* This spiritual work of mercy is a biggie! It might very well be the most challenging one of all. When it comes to forgiveness, I like what J. V. Taylor said: "Forgiveness grasps the searing stone of sin and will not pass it on."

7. *Pray for the living and the dead.* Throughout Scripture we are encouraged to pray for others—both the living and the dead. This final spiritual work of mercy, then, is based on the belief in the communion of saints. This means a marvelous bond unites all humankind—both those who have already gone before us into eternal life and those who now share this life on earth with us. This work of mercy encourages us to expand the boundaries of our prayer, which also might expand the boundaries of our love.

What evidence is there in my life that I practice these spiritual works of mercy?

Loving God, help me to live these spiritual works of mercy in my everyday life.

34 On Modesty

The proud person counts his newspaper clippings—the humble
person his blessings.
—Fulton J. Sheen

Rice

> *Some foods don't mind being cooked in full view:*
> *like eggs frying, pasta boiling, or chicken on the grill.*
> *But not so rice. Rice likes privacy.*
> *It demands a cover while it simmers in the pot,*
> *warning, "No fair peeking till I'm through!"*
> *(And you'd better not, too!)*
> *In a world where privacy is rare,*
> *modesty mocked, and unpretentiousness unheard of,*
> *it's nice to know there are still some things*
> *like rice.*

My poem is not really about rice, of course. It is about modesty. Now, as soon as I say the word *modesty*, some of us immediately think of clothing. We think modesty is what you do not have if your hemline is too high or your neckline is too low. Or sometimes we equate modesty with shyness or bashfulness. Wallflowers at dances are modest, we say. But modesty is more than how much cleavage you do not show or how far you slink from the dance floor. Modesty is a gift of the Spirit.

The word *modesty* comes from the Latin word *modestus* which means "keeping due measure." Modest people are individuals who keep good measure. They are good at measuring the worth and the extent of things. Their measuring begins with themselves. Modest people have a sense of their own personal worth.

> Modest people are individuals who keep good measure. They are good at measuring the worth and the extent of things.

Modest people also know that not everything has to be made public. Unfortunately, we live in a culture that thrives on publicizing just about everything down to the most intimate details of a person's life. Some of this publicity is uninvited and downright intrusive. But some of it is actually welcomed and cultivated. Someone who seeks such publicity is certainly not modest.

Jesus calls us to modesty. He reminds us of our glory, "You are worth more than many sparrows" (Luke 12:7), and of our limitations, "Can you by worrying add a single moment to your life-span?" (Matthew 6:27). He tells us to keep some things private: "When you pray, go to your inner room, close the door, and pray to your Father in secret" (Matthew 6:6). And again, "When you give alms, do not let your left hand know what your right is doing" (Matthew 6:3). Now that is modesty—according to Jesus.

How modest am I? Do I have a good sense of my talents and limitations? Do I have a healthy sense of privacy?

Jesus, help me to go to my inner room, close the door, and pray to God in secret today.

35 On Mystery

It is easier for us to say what God is not, than what God is.
—St. Augustine

A mystery is something that baffles us, something beyond our comprehension. There are mysteries (small letter) and there are Mysteries (capital letter). Small mysteries include things like: "Where's my other sock?" "What ever possessed you to do such a thing?" "Is there really a Loch Ness monster?" Big Mysteries include things like these: "Why was I born at this time and in this place?" "What makes two people fall in love?" "Why do bad things happen to good people?" As humans, we tend to be uncomfortable with mysteries. We seem to have this innate need to define, control, and own things. Mysteries, however, refuse to be defined, controlled, and owned by anyone—including us. They elude our manipulation—and this can be good news for our souls.

Every time we encounter Mystery, we touch the fringes of God's robe. (I'm speaking metaphorically, of course.) In a way, every Mystery we meet helps prepare us for encountering God, the greatest Mystery of all. The fact is, the more we know God, the more we know how little we know God. This sense of God's incomprehensibility was the experience of many of the saints. St. Thomas Aquinas, for example, spent his whole life theologizing and writing about God. His massive *Summa Theologica* has been called the most extensive and systematic exposition of the faith ever written. But toward the end of his life, Thomas had some sort of mystical encounter with God that caused him to retire his pen forever. When

> *The fact is, the more we know God, the more we know how little we know God.*

questioned why he was no longer writing he said, "I cannot go on. . . . All I have written seems to me like so much straw compared to what I have seen and what has been revealed to me." For Thomas, a whole lifetime of studying and writing about God was nothing compared to one second of actually seeing God.

In his book *The Trivialization of God*, Donald McCullough reminds us how important it is to respect the incomprehensibility of God. The God of Scripture, he says, is not a household pet or warm and fuzzy. Rather God is "wholly other, radically different from anything else in creation, terrifying in greatness, and utterly awesome in love."

Mystery is good for the soul. Mystery is also a very good name for God.

How do I experience God's incomprehensibility? Do I ever try to control or manipulate God?

Incomprehensible God, help me to experience your terrifying greatness and your utterly awesome love today.

36 On Patience

Time and I can take on any two.
—Proverb

When I hear the word *saint,* the first image that comes to my mind is not some Carmelite nun kneeling in a darkened chapel fingering her rosary beads. Now, I am sure many Carmelite nuns are saints, but they are not the first things I think of.

The first image that comes to my mind is a young mother in the parking lot at the mall, trying to get three children—all under five—into their car seats. It reminds me of someone trying to put an octopus to bed. The woman gets the first child buckled in his seat when the second one starts to scream, "Cookie! Cookie!" The woman digs into a grocery bag, rips open a box of cookies, and shoves one at the kid. Then she lifts him into his car seat. That's when the first kid starts screaming that he wants a cookie, too. She fishes around for a cookie for him. Meanwhile the baby, who is still in the stroller, starts fussing, so, after giving a cookie to the first child, the woman turns her attention to the third. That's when the second child starts hitting the first one with the cookie box, and the first one starts to cry. Even when the woman has succeeded, by some miracle, in getting all three children into their car seats, she is not finished yet. She still has to put the shopping bags in the car, collapse the stroller, lift it into the back, and get herself into the car, too. And when she gets home, she has got to reverse the whole process. Now that is sanctity!

It is also tremendous patience—and patience is yet another gift of the Holy Spirit. The word *patience* is derived from the Latin verb *passio,* meaning "to bear or endure." Patient people are those who can bear trials and pains with calmness and equanimity. They are able to put up with delays, wait for the right moment, and bide their time.

Patient people are more flexible with time than impatient people. Impatient people exist in only one time frame—their own. They are comfortable with only one schedule—theirs. They want things done when they want things done. And they expect the rest of the world to adapt to their schedule. If they want their child to be potty trained by twenty-four months and he is not by twenty-six, they get angry. If they have to stand in line at the store while an elderly lady ahead of them carries on a brief conversation with the cashier, they get upset because that lady is disrupting their schedule.

> *Patient people are those who can bear trials and pains with calmness and equanimity.*

Patient people, on the other hand, can flow back and forth between different time frames. They know, for example, that potty training a child may necessitate entering a time frame other than their own. Waiting in line for a few extra moments while an elderly lady chats with a cashier invites patient people to momentarily set aside their own schedule. They enter with compassion the schedule of another, someone who is lonely and who may have more time than she knows what to do with.

Recently I did some creative imaging and took a walk with Patience. When I asked her, "What can I do to become more like you?" she thought for a moment, smiled warmly, and said, "Plant an acorn. . . . Befriend a turtle. . . . Teach a child."

How patient am I? Am I able to step out of my own time frame and enter with compassion the time frame of someone else?

God of infinite patience, let me walk with you today.

37 On Piety

Nowhere does the Torah say, "Invite your guest to pray"; but it does tell us to offer a guest food, drink, and a bed.
—Jewish Proverb

I used to think a pious person was someone who genuflected profoundly before getting into a pew, closed her eyes during prayer, and lit a lot of candles in church. In other words, piety to me meant the performing of external religious practices. But then I learned that the scriptural meaning of piety goes far beyond that. In Scripture, the word for piety is *hesed*, "which means compassionate goodness." *Hesed* begins with God's compassionate goodness to us. To Moses, God says, "[I am] a merciful and gracious God, slow to anger and rich in kindness and fidelity" (Exodus 34:6). That's *hesed*.

God's compassionate goodness toward us calls for a similar response of love on our part—not only to God, but also to our neighbor. In Scripture, true piety is always associated with justice toward others. Perhaps there is no finer expression of piety than these words of the prophet Micah: "This is what the Lord asks of you: only this, to act justly, to love tenderly, and to walk humbly with your God" (Micah 6:8). Let's look at those three phrases.

To act justly. In their letter "Economic Justice for All," the United States Conference of Catholic Bishops writes, "The quest for justice rises from loving gratitude for the saving acts of God and manifests itself in the wholehearted love of God and neighbor." Three words stand out for me in that sentence: *quest*, *gratitude*, and *wholehearted*. The bishops use the phrase "quest for justice," reminding us that justice is not something we have already achieved, but something we must continuously strive for. The bishops also say that "justice rises from loving gratitude for the saving acts of God." If we are in touch with the saving acts of God, we will be grateful. It is as simple as that. But we express our gratitude to God not primarily by saying prayers of thanksgiving, but by working for the promotion of justice for all.

To love tenderly. In their pastoral letter, the bishops also describe the kind of love we are to have for God and neighbor—wholehearted. What does wholehearted love look like? It is a love that is sincere, all-inclusive, enthusiastic, dynamic, impassioned, determined, unreserved. In short, it is the kind of love Jesus showed to the people he ministered to—individuals like the stooped woman, the man with a withered hand, the Roman centurion, the adulterous woman, the little children, the ten lepers, and the multitudes hungry for more than mere earthly bread.

The gift of piety, then, does more than light candles. It inflames our hearts.

To walk humbly with your God. This phrase conjures up images of God walking with Adam and Eve in the garden in the cool of the evening. Or of Jesus calmly strolling across the water past his apostles in their boat. Or of Jesus nonchalantly joining the two downcast disciples on their way to Emmaus. The gift of piety, then, does more than light candles. It inflames our hearts.

How faithful am I to my religious duty of loving God and my neighbor?

Loving God, help me to act justly, love tenderly, and walk humbly with you today.

38 On Pleasure

A person will be called to account on Judgment Day for every permissible thing he or she might have enjoyed but did not.
—Talmud

When we hear the word *pleasure*, we are more likely to think not of virtue but of sin—more particularly the so-called capital sins: gluttony, lust, sloth. Be honest, when was the last time you heard a sermon proclaiming the merits of bodily pleasures? When was the last time you asked God to increase your capacity for pleasure? Let's face it, when it comes to promoting pleasure, Christianity has a pretty bad track record. We are much more apt to surround pleasure with red flares than we are to present her with red roses.

_____
God is the ultimate source of all pleasure.
_____

That is unfortunate. After all, where did pleasure come from? That's right, from God. God is the ultimate source of all pleasure. When I taught human sexuality to high school kids, I used to write in big letters on the board: REMEMBER: GOD INVENTED SEX! Sometimes that sentence would blow their minds!

How can we grow in our acceptance of, and appreciation for, pleasure? We can begin by becoming more aware of the built-in pleasures of our daily life. For example, eating is meant to be pleasurable. What can we do to enhance the pleasure of eating? Maybe we need to make time for eating. Rather than zapping boxed meals in the microwave, we could take time to prepare a meal from scratch—at least on a more regular basis. Instead of shoving a piece of pizza into our mouths as we race out the door, we could take the time to sit down and eat, savoring our meal—as well as the company with whom we eat. Maybe it also means eating what is good for us, so we do not nullify the pleasure of eating with the pain of indigestion or ill health.

There is a story told about St. Teresa of Ávila, that great mystic and doctor of the Church. It seems her sisters were scandalized one day when they saw Teresa gorging on roast partridge. Sensing their shock, Teresa said to them cheerfully, "At prayer time, pray! At partridge time, partridge!"

Sleep is another pleasure God has invented for us. Do we get enough sleep? Do we deal with problems during the day that might interfere with this pleasure at night? We might even want to take a "Pleasure Inventory" and list those things that ordinarily bring us pleasure. Here are some of mine: listening to music, playing the piano, phoning a friend, watching birds, swimming, going for a walk, working crossword puzzles, ice-skating, playing with a child, reading a good book, hanging out with friends. The list goes on and on. Once we have our list, we can ask ourselves, "When was the last time I did any of these things?" Maybe we have to program pleasure into our pleasure-deprived existence!

One cold February I was feeling depressed. I was dealing with some personal problems at the time, so I attributed my depression to that. But, through a casual conversation with a friend, I suddenly realized that I, unknowingly, had not been doing any of those things I really enjoyed doing—those things that gave me pleasure. So what did I do? The next day I laced up my ice skates and skated on a pond for an hour. It helped. Pleasure can do that for us.

What is my basic attitude toward pleasure? What does my "Pleasure Inventory" say to me?

God, source of all pleasure, increase my capacity and appreciation for pleasure.

39 On Prophecy

The prophets were drunk on God, and in the presence of their terrible tipsiness, no one was ever comfortable.
—Frederick Buechner

When we hear the word *prophet*, we usually think of someone who predicts the future. But that's not what prophets did in the Bible, at least, not primarily. A prophet was God's spokesperson, God's mouthpiece. Oh sure, sometimes they said things about the future, but most of the time they talked about the present—which they knew exceptionally well. More often than not, the prophets told people that they were misbehaving and that God was displeased with their misbehaving. Most prophets didn't choose to be prophets. They didn't apply for the job. In fact, some went to great lengths to avoid being prophets.

The prophets' reluctance to prophesy stemmed from the fact that prophecy was a dangerous profession, one that merited this label: *WARNING: Prophesying can be hazardous to your health!* The prophets, as a rule, were treated terribly. Jeremiah was thrown into a cistern. Elijah was chased hither and yon by the wicked queen Jezebel. His life became so unbearable, he begged God for death on more than one occasion. But God always said, "Not yet."

In addition to being reluctant, the prophets were also a little strange. They weren't the type of individuals you'd invite to your dinner party. But despite their idiosyncrasies, the prophets were a courageous lot. Take the prophet Nathan. He had the gall to tell King David, to his face, that he was a cheat, a liar, an adulterer, and a murderer! David really was all those things, but fortunately for Nathan, he was also repentant. Instead of killing Nathan on the spot, David admitted his sins and turned his life around. All thanks to the courageous prophet.

Jesus was something of a prophet, although he never claimed the title for himself. He did some strange things—like giving up a fairly secure job as a carpenter to become an itinerant preacher with no pay. He was God's mouthpiece, calling people to repentance and assuring them of God's unfailing love. He was courageous, standing up to opposition even when he needed no crystal ball to see where it was leading him. And, of course, Jesus suffered immeasurably—probably more than any of the prophets before him.

What does prophecy have to do with us? Like the prophets, we also can offer advice when we are asked—rather than act as if we haven't learned anything from our own prayer and experience that might be helpful to others. We can imitate the prophets' ability to console and encourage others, for that was one of their major tasks. Finally, we, like the prophets, can care. We can care about our families, friends, community, parish, church, and world. We can care enough to speak God's truth.

Like the prophets, we also can offer advice when we are asked—rather than act as if we haven't learned anything from our own prayer and experience that might be helpful to others.

Do I always speak the truth even when it is hard to do so? Whom have I consoled and encouraged lately?

Spirit of Jesus, fill me with your truth.

40 On Relaxation

The challenge of being human is so great, no one gets it right every time.
—Rabbi Harold Kushner

One of my favorite cartoons shows two snakes. One is resting on the ground, his body relaxed in supple curves. The other is leaning against a tree, his body stiff and straight as a board. The one on the ground says to the other, "Charlie, you've gotta learn to relax already!" Many of us need to hear the words, "Relax already!" We might be more inclined to actually relax if we were convinced that relaxation is, indeed, a gift of the Holy Spirit.

Let's begin by looking at the main enemy of relaxation: perfectionism. Many people cannot relax because they are trying too hard to be perfect. Perfectionists are people who put excessive demands upon themselves—and sometimes upon others as well. Psychiatrists say that perfectionism is often a way of compensating for low self-esteem. It can also arise from repressed fears of abandonment or shame.

> *Many people cannot relax because they are trying too hard to be perfect.*

In her book *Bird by Bird*, Anne Lamott calls perfectionism "the voice of the oppressor." She continues, "Perfectionism is based on the obsessive belief that if you run carefully enough, hitting each stepping-stone just right, you won't have to die." She concludes, "The truth is you will die anyway and a lot of people who aren't even looking at their feet are going to do a lot better than you, and have a lot more fun while they're doing it."

Both perfectionism and our ability to relax are directly linked to our image of God. If we believe God is sitting up in heaven with a clipboard, carefully noting our every failing, then we can easily become perfectionists. If, on the other hand, we believe God loves us immensely and is walking beside us, whispering in our ear, "Don't be afraid. Nothing can happen that you and I can't handle together," then we can readily afford to relax.

Jesus knew how to relax. He frequented the home of Mary, Martha, and Lazarus, for example, not to preach to them, but to relax with them. In their home in Bethany, Jesus was able to kick his feet up and let his hair down. We sense that Jesus knew how to relax when we read his parables. How did he come up with such effective images for his parables—bread rising, seeds germinating, camels squeezing through narrow gates, wayward sons returning home—except that he took the time to observe the world around him, to converse with people, and to reflect upon his own lived experience? He could do that because he knew how to relax.

Not only did Jesus himself relax, he also told his disciples to relax on numerous occasions. "Come away by yourselves to a deserted place and rest a while," he said to the Twelve when they returned from their exhausting speaking engagements (Mark 6:31). Other times he said to his listeners things like, "Don't worry . . . don't be afraid . . . stop fretting." Why? "Because God loves you like there's no tomorrow," and "Because everything ultimately is in God's hands."

Am I ever a perfectionist? What helps me to relax?

Holy Spirit, bless me with the grace to relax today.

41 On Responsibility

If not us, who? If not now, when?
—Slogan of Czech university students in Prague, 1989

In his book *World of Stories for Preachers and Teachers*, William Bausch tells this little-known fact about riding in a stagecoach in the Old West. The stagecoach had three kinds of tickets: first class, second class, and third class. If you had a first class ticket, you were allowed to remain seated the entire trip, no matter what happened. If the stagecoach got stuck in the mud, or had trouble going up a steep hill, or even if one of its wheels fell off, you could remain seated. If you had a second class ticket, you could remain seated until there was a problem. In that case, you had to get off the stagecoach until the problem was solved. You could stand around and watch as others fixed the problem. You yourself did not have to actually get your hands dirty, and as soon as the problem was fixed, you were allowed to get back into your seat. If you had a third class ticket, you had to get off the stagecoach if there was a problem because it was your responsibility to help fix the problem. This meant you had to get out and push the stagecoach out of the mud, or up the hill, or even help fix a broken wheel.

After hearing this, we might ask ourselves, "On the stagecoach journey of life, what kind of ticket am I holding?" A first class ticket? That means if there is a problem, I do nothing about it. In fact, others have to work around me. A second class ticket? That means I watch others try to fix life's problems. Or a third class ticket? That means I sense it is partly my responsibility to help fix the problems encountered along the journey of life.

I believe that we, as Christians, hold third class tickets on the stagecoach of life. We are called to help solve life's problems. In fact, assuming that responsibility is what discipleship is all about.

The big question to ask ourselves is "for what or for whom do I feel responsible?" Some people feel responsible only for themselves. This excessive individualism is in the very air that we breathe. Other individuals feel responsible only for their immediate family or their little circle of friends. The rest of the world can go to pot as far as they're concerned. Still others feel responsible only for their local community, their parish, their particular ethnic group. They see no connection between their local community and the larger global community.

But through the gift of responsibility, the Spirit is forever trying to enlarge the sweep of our love, reminding us that we are part of something more important than our individual selves, more expansive than our family circle. We are members of a community, a church, a nation, a world. As such, we must continuously work to further the coming of God's Kingdom. That is our responsibility. That is our call.

> *Through the gift of responsibility, the Spirit is forever trying to enlarge the sweep of our love.*

For what or for whom do I have a responsibility? How may the Spirit be calling me to expand the sweep of my love?

Jesus, help me to see more clearly my responsibility for furthering God's Kingdom in my time and place.

42 On Sickness

In life as in dance: Grace glides on blistered feet.
—Alice Abrams

Last year I learned I had a rare disease called *polymyositis*, a condition where the auto-immune system begins to attack and destroy healthy cells in the body. The symptoms include painful swelling, general fatigue, and muscle weakness. There is no cure for polymyositis. In fact, twenty percent of the people with the disease die within five years. Others, however, go on to live long lives by managing the illness with medication.

Some people believe that God sends us illness for a specific purpose. I have heard people say, "God gave me cancer so I would appreciate my family more." "God gave me a heart attack so I would slow down." Others maintain that sickness makes us special. When hearing of my diagnosis, someone said to me, "God must love you very much." But I don't believe that God sends us illness to get our attention or to teach us a particular lesson. Nor do I believe that sickness makes us special. Rather, I believe illness is a part of the human condition. Nothing more, nothing less. But what we do with illness, how we face it, is what really matters. When we view illness through the eyes of faith, it can be a gift of the Holy Spirit.

A few months after learning I had polymyositis, I made my annual retreat. I was looking for answers to the questions many people ask when confronted with serious sickness. Why did I get this sickness? Will I die from it? If so, how soon? Where is God in all of this?

I didn't find answers to all of my questions during retreat. In prayer, however, I did arrive at this simple statement: *God is with me in this.* I found myself repeating these words over and over again, sensing that

God was with me now in this illness, and he would be with me in the future—whatever that future might hold. I also found myself saying, "God is *in* me *with* this. God is somehow present in me during this illness just as God has always been present in me in the past. And God will continue to be present in me until death calls me home." I found this realization immensely consoling and encouraging.

Sickness can be a gift of the Holy Spirit—if we allow it to be. It can be a wonderful teacher if we are willing to be its disciple. The writer Flannery O'Connor, who suffered the debilitating effects of lupus for many years, wrote, "Sickness is a place, more instructive than a long trip to Europe." Yes, sickness can be instructive. It can teach us to be more compassionate, to slow down, to treasure our loved ones more, to get our priorities straight, to appreciate the gift of life more, and to humbly acknowledge our need for others—especially for God.

> *Sickness can be a gift of the Holy Spirit—if we allow it to be. It can be a wonderful teacher if we are willing to be its disciple.*

How has my sickness or the sickness of someone else been instructive for me?

Loving God, I believe you are with me in this—whatever that "this" might be.

43 On Song

"How can I keep from singing?"
—Traditional hymn

Aldous Huxley wrote, "After silence, that which comes nearest to expressing the inexpressible is music." Throughout scripture, God commanded the Israelites to sing. Maybe one reason God did this is because song or music is so much like God, the Inexpressible One. In fact, in the Bible, God and song go hand in hand. Whenever God pays a visit to people in Scripture, they often

> Whenever God pays a visit to people in Scripture, they often end up singing.

end up singing. When God parted the Red Sea, and the Israelites marched through it without a trace of mud on their sandals, what was the first thing they did? That's right, they sang: "Then Moses and the Israelites sang this song to the LORD: I will sing to the LORD, for he is gloriously triumphant; horse and chariot he has cast into the sea" (Exodus 15:1). When Hannah gave birth to little Samuel, the answer to her prayer, she too broke out into song: "My heart exults in the LORD, my horn is exalted in my God" (1 Samuel 2:1). When Mary visited Elizabeth, she sang her famous aria, the Magnificat: "The Mighty One has done great things for me, and holy is his name" (Luke 1:49). It's as if, when we humans detect that God is near, we can't help but break out into song.

Jesus probably sang. Like most children of his time, he would have learned his first songs from his parents. We can imagine Jesus going to the synagogue as a child, and listening with rapt attention (or squirming with childish impatience) at the canting of the sacred texts during Sabbath prayer. As an adult, Jesus, in all likelihood, did not merely recite the psalms, he probably sang them—as they were meant to be prayed. And at the Last Supper, it is not far-fetched to suppose that Jesus sang even the sacred words we now use at the consecration: "This is my body . . . this is my blood . . . do this in memory of me."

The poet Thomas Carlyle said music was the "speech of angels." Henry Wadsworth Longfellow, too, saw a direct link between faith and song. He called song "the Prophet's art" and added that "Among the gifts that God hath sent," music is "one of the most magnificent." It is only fitting, then, that we conclude this reflection on the gift of song with this melodic message of the prophet, Isaiah, who said (or perhaps sang) these words: "The Lord is my salvation. The Lord is my strength and my song" (Isaiah 12:2).

What role do song and music play in my life? In my prayer?

God, source of all music, make my life a song for you.

44 On Stability

Stability has far more to do with honesty than it does with one's
zip code.
—Demetrius Dumm, OSB

When I was a little girl, I sometimes misbehaved. People who know me well will not be surprised. When I was bad, my mother had an effective way of disciplining me. She did not scream or spank me. Instead, she pointed to one of the chairs in the dining room and said, "Sit, until I tell you that you can move." Now, sitting still in one place was pure torture for me. Although I seldom had to sit there for more than a few minutes, those few minutes dragged on and on until I was sure I had been sitting on that chair for a hundred years! Sometimes, if I detected my mother was in a negotiable mood, I would plead with her to please let me get off the chair, adding with as much sincerity as I could muster, "I'll be good! I promise!"

Staying in one place is hard not only for children, but also for adults. We humans have an innate affinity for movement. Isn't this why babies like to be rocked, why we find cars so appealing, and why we can stare for hours at a river flowing by? So when I say stability is one of the gifts of the Spirit, some might say, "You're kidding, aren't you?" No, I am not kidding. But first let's explore what stability as a gift of the Spirit really means.

Stability does not simply mean staying in one place—although it can include that. More accurately, stability means not running away from the self-knowledge that we can gain only through interaction with others. We will be tempted to run away because self-knowledge can hurt. Over the years, I have devised a little practice that helps me deal with the pain of self-knowledge. When, usually through interaction with others, I come face to face with a shortcoming of mine, I say to myself, "Ouch!" In other words, "Ouch! I'm not as kind as I thought I was." "Ouch! I'm not as responsible as I imagined." "Ouch! I'm not as loving as I assumed." For some strange reason, saying ouch to myself lessens the pain of the moment—much like a woman who (more intensely, of course!) screams during childbirth. The childbirth analogy, by the way, is a good one because every moment of honest self-knowledge can be a moment of birth.

Stability means not running away from the self-knowledge we can gain only through interaction with others.

But self-knowledge is not always painful. Sometimes it is downright pleasurable. Honest self-knowledge includes those good things about ourselves that we can only learn from others: "You're really thoughtful." "I get a kick out of you." "I admire your courage." "Thanks for making me laugh." Stability prevents us from running away from our virtues as well as our vices. It also means never brushing off a compliment.

Rabbi Hillel, a first-century Jewish teacher, gave this advice: "Do not withdraw from community." Stability is the gift that keeps us rooted in community and, as such, rooted in the truth of who we are.

Do I ever run away from the self-knowledge I can gain only through interaction with others? Do I brush off compliments?

God, give me the gift of stability that I may more willingly grow in self-knowledge.

45 On Surrender

Surrender is yielding to God's dream for us.
—James Krisher

For many of us, the word *surrender* conjures up only negative images. Even the synonyms we use for surrender reinforce this negativity: to give up, to abandon, to buckle under, to hand over, to eat humble pie, to cave in, to quit.

Another reason the word *surrender* is so pejorative is because of the highly competitive society in which we live. It is forever telling us that winning is everything. It teaches us to control, to dominate, and—above all—to never give up! Even if we do not see surrender as cowardly, we tend to view it as passive. Surrender means to accept things as they are, to go with the flow, to adopt a *que sera, sera* attitude. If all of this is true, then how in the world can we say that surrender is a gift of the Holy Spirit?

James Krisher has written a book entitled *Spiritual Surrender: Yielding Yourself to a Loving God*. In it, he says that spiritual surrender—that is, yielding to God—is anything but wimpish or passive. Spiritual surrender takes great courage and resolve. Krisher describes such surrender as "an active choice to place our person, forces, and possessions into the hands of God." Such surrender is always life-giving.

Imagine placing our person, forces, and possessions into God's hands. Our faith tradition is replete with individuals who surrendered to God in that fashion and, by doing so, found abundant new life—not only for themselves, but for others. Moses surrendered to God at the burning bush and went on to deliver the Israelites from slavery. Jonah surrendered to God in the belly of the whale and saved the Ninevites from destruction. Mary surrendered to God at the

Annunciation and gave birth to the Messiah. Paul surrendered to God on the road to Damascus and became the great apostle to the Gentiles. Ignatius surrendered to God on a sick bed and went on to found a congregation that has served the church for over 450 years. Sojourner Truth surrendered to God in 1843 and became one of the most influential voices against the evils of slavery.

Spiritual surrender is not always easy or neat. It is seldom once-and-for-all, either. Our God is a God who calls us again and again. Like a persistent lover, God pursues, charms, and woos us. The prophet Jeremiah experienced firsthand the irresistible attractiveness of God. He describes his own spiritual surrender in these memorable words: "Oh Lord, you have enticed me, and I was enticed; you have overpowered me, and you have prevailed" (Jeremiah 20:7).

Spiritual surrender is not always easy or neat. It is seldom once-and-for-all, either.

It is my guess that those of you reading this book have already experienced something of spiritual surrender. Hopefully, having tasted the new life that such surrender brings, you (like me) desire only to surrender ever more completely to our God, the Divine Lover.

Have I ever experienced spiritual surrender? What holds me back from surrendering more completely to God?

God, you have enticed me. Help me to surrender more completely to your dream for me.

46 On Truth

The truth will set you free.
—John 8:32

Here is the truth about Truth.

Truth is not the same as *facts*. Facts tell us what things are. Truth reveals to us what things mean. There are many kinds of truth: mathematical, scientific, theological, philosophical, poetic, psychological. Truth can never be limited to just one of these kinds. Nor can one kind of truth be held superior to another. There can be just as much truth in a poem, for instance, as there is in a scientific formula. Ultimately, Truth is all of these kinds of truth together. Also, Truth can go wherever she wants. She can show up in a science lab, a church, a courtroom, an assembly line, a classroom, a bedroom—provided she is invited. Sometimes she even shows up uninvited. Although Truth is comfortable with everyone, she seems especially at home with children and the dying.

Truth is not always obvious. She tends to be shyer than Deceit, more reserved than Dishonesty. Truth is far more careful and attentive than Inaccuracy, too. That's one reason she gets around more slowly than Falsehood. As Mark Twain said, "A lie can travel around the world before the truth even puts on her shoes!" Some people are strangers to Truth; others are bosom friends with her. But still, no one knows her completely. As the old proverb warns, "Align yourself with the person who seeks the truth, but run away from the one who claims to have found it!"

We do not always see Truth clearly. Sometimes that's because Truth is difficult to decipher, but more often it is because we are more comfortable not seeing her. Truth can sting or hurt—terribly. So we say things like, "There's nothing wrong with my marriage." "My kid is not on drugs." "I am not lonely." "Everything's fine!" To admit otherwise would inflict pain too great for us to bear—or so we imagine. If only we would realize that, ultimately, the pain that Truth can bring is never as great as the pain of living without her. What's more, Truth's pain is only temporary. It eventually leaves, making room for the other friends Truth always brings with her: Humility, Trust, Forgiveness, and Freedom.

> *The pain that Truth can bring is never as great as the pain of living without her.*

St. Thomas Aquinas said that falsehood is never so false as when it is nearly true. It is never so dangerous, either. For a near-truth (or a half-truth) can inflict far more damage than a whole lie. That's because we are taken in more easily by a half-truth than a complete falsehood.

In the end, there are these two: Love and Truth, standing together, their arms forever linked. Neither can live without the other. Truth without Love is empty. Love without Truth is an illusion.

This is the truth about Truth, but, of course, not the whole truth.

What has been my experience of Truth? Have I ever experienced her pain or her freedom?

Jesus, you are the truth. Help me to align myself with truth today and every day.

47 On Understanding

Jesus summoned the crowd and said to them, "Hear and understand."
—Matthew 15:10

Understanding is the ability to crawl into another person's skin. It means to walk a mile in their moccasins—or high heels, or sandals, or sneakers, or cowboy boots, or bare feet. It means to see things from

> Understanding is the ability to crawl into another person's skin.

their perspective, to sense how they feel. Understanding is a close relative of compassion. In fact, it is often difficult to tell where one ends and the other begins

Understanding demands detachment. It means that I must let go of my own way of looking at things—at least temporarily—in order to take up someone else's way of perceiving reality. If I am Tom, a middle-aged white man in Boston, and I'm trying to understand Latisha, a young African-American woman in Atlanta, then I must let go of my middle-agedness, my whiteness, my maleness, and even Boston-ness to begin to understand Latisha. If Latisha wants to understand Tom, then she must do the same kind of letting go. This is no small feat. In fact, some would argue that it is downright impossible to let go of so much in order to embrace another's reality. Understanding understands this, but still says, "Try it! Make the effort at least! Take one baby-step toward knowing and appreciating another, and you'll see, you'll see!"

Understanding requires humility. It concedes, "My perception is incomplete. My world is not the whole world. There are other ways of doing things, other values and experiences that are just as valid as my own." And understanding means it, too.

The opposite of understanding is a judgmental attitude. Understanding takes time. Judgmental people, on the other hand, are usually in a rush. Rather than take the time to get to know people, they take the shortcut and judge them. Judgmental people are not only in a hurry, they are often fearful, too. The prospect of letting go of their world—their ideas, opinions, habits, and value systems—terrifies them. They find it hard to understand why anyone would ever want to do such a thing. Judgmental individuals sometimes lack imagination. This makes it hard for them to envision how others think or feel. (I hope I haven't been too judgmental of judgmental people!)

The gift of understanding is sorely needed in a world such as ours, a world marked by excessive individualism, growing mistrust, accelerating violence, and *ism's* of all kinds: racism, nationalism, sexism, ageism. As such, the gift of understanding plays not a cameo role in our lives as Christians; rather it has a leading role in bringing about the Kingdom of God here on earth. If only we would understand that better!

What evidence do I give of having received the gift of understanding? Is there any evidence that I am judgmental?

God of understanding, help me to crawl into someone else's skin today.

48 On Whimsy

If it looks like fun and doesn't break the Ten Commandments, do it.
—Karol A. Jackowski

The word *whimsy* can mean several things. It can mean something fanciful or odd. It connotes unpredictable behavior or erratic change. But it is most appropriate for religious discussions, because it captures what can happen when God pays us a visit. We can become whimsical—that is, we can change. Our behavior can become unpredictable. We may even be thought odd or mentally unbalanced by others.

Scripture presents us with a slew of whimsical people, but one of my favorites is Hannah, the mother of Samuel (1 Samuel 1:1–28). Hannah was married to Elkanah, who had another wife named Peninnah. Hannah was as barren as a rock, whereas Peninnah was as fertile as a turtle. Day after day Peninnah mocked Hannah for her barrenness. Poor Elkanah must have had his hands full. But the story says that he clearly favored Hannah, despite her childlessness.

Year after year, Hannah made a pilgrimage to the sanctuary of the Lord, begging God to send her a son. But it seemed to no avail. One day she went to the sanctuary and threw herself on the floor, flooding the place with her tears. Rocking back and forth, she cried in her heart to God, "If you give me a son, I'll give him right back to you, to serve you in the temple. I promise!" What a whimsical thing to say!

Eli, a priest of God, saw Hannah groveling in the sanctuary. He thought, "That woman's plastered!" and stomped over to restore respectability to the holy place. He scolded her severely, but Hannah explained the reason for her strange behavior, sharing with him the agony that caused her tears and wailing. Eli, himself well acquainted with pain, listened attentively and told her finally, "Go in peace. And may God grant you your request." That's all Hannah needed to hear. She picked herself up, went home and, after a few nights of love-making with Elkanah (the Bible is very clear about that!), she conceived a child. Finally! Nine months later she gave birth to Samuel.

As soon as little Samuel was weaned, Hannah plopped him in his stroller, packed him a suitcase, grabbed her husband, and they all marched off to the temple to make the customary offering to God. When it came time to leave, Hannah did the seemingly impossible. She handed her son to Eli, saying, "Here, he's yours." Or, more accurately, "Here, he is God's." She gave her son to the service of God in the temple—as she had promised even before he was conceived. Isn't that strange? She who begged and begged for a son and now had him, was giving him up! Talk about whimsy! But the best whimsy is yet to come.

As Hannah and Elkanah left the temple, Hannah was filled with the spirit of God and sang out a magnificent hymn of thanksgiving. "My heart exults in the Lord," she cried. She proceeded to describe a world made topsy-turvy by a God who seems to delight in surprise and the unexpected. "The bows of the mighty are broken, while the tottering gird on strength. The well-fed hire themselves out for bread, while the hungry fatten on spoil." On and on, this possessed woman sang the praises of a whimsical God *On and on, this possessed woman sang the praises of a whimsical God who refused to be held back by the limits of our human expectations.* who refused to be held back by the limits of our human expectations.

Many years later, another woman named Mary, full of whimsy as well, echoed Hannah's words. Only her child was no ordinary child. He would be Jesus, the Son of God.

Do I have any whimsy? Have I ever been visited by the whimsical God?

God of whimsy, visit me and break through the limits of my human expectations.

49 On Wisdom

When wisdom enters, subtlety comes along.
—Talmud

Wisdom is the gift of the Spirit that tells us how to live. It reveals to us the nature of reality and directs us to live our lives in accord with that reality. Wisdom tells us what is true, right, and lasting. It helps us to discern values, enter into relationships, and make good judgments.

But there are different kinds of wisdom. One kind is human wisdom, or conventional wisdom. Human wisdom says things like, "Love your friends, but hate your enemies." "The important thing is the bottom line." "Winning is everything." But Christians believe in a wisdom derived from the teachings of Jesus. This wisdom says, "Love your friends and your enemies." "The important thing is compassion." "Loving, not winning, is everything." In short, not everything that looks like wisdom really is.

This idea is brought out in Marcus Borg's book *Meeting Jesus Again for the First Time.* Borg devotes two chapters to a discussion of Jesus and wisdom. He begins by saying that Jesus was, above all, a teacher of wisdom, a sage. But Jesus' wisdom was often in opposition to the conventional wisdom of his day. We can see this in Jesus' aphorisms (those great one-liners) and in his parables (those great short stories).

The Gospels record over a hundred of Jesus' aphorisms. For example: "You cannot serve two masters." "The last shall be first." "You strain out a gnat and swallow a camel." "If a blind person leads a blind person, will they not both fall into a ditch?" All of his aphorisms invite his listeners to see something in a new way. As Borg says, "they tease the imagination into activity, suggest more than they say, and invite a transformation of perception." We might add that Jesus' aphorisms lead to a new kind of wisdom.

Let's look at one of those aphorisms: "You strain out a gnat and swallow a camel." These words were directed toward the Pharisees, who emphasized legal purity in a big way. Though the image is humorous, the point is serious: how foolish it is to strain out something teeny weeny, while swallowing something humongous. Jesus' words invite his listeners (and us!) to raise these questions: "Do I ever do something as foolish as this?" "What are the gnats and camels in my life?" "What is the relationship between religious practices and religion itself?"

Another way Jesus set forth his wisdom was through his parables. Notice, however, that Jesus did not force his wisdom onto anyone. In fact, he often began his stories with phrases like: "Judge for yourself what is right" or "What do you think?" As Borg says, his style of delivery "was invitational rather than imperative."

For Christians, the ultimate wisdom, of course, is the folly of the cross. St. Paul says this well when he writes to the Corinthians, "Has not God made the wisdom of the world foolish? . . . But we proclaim Christ crucified, a stumbling block to [many] . . . For the foolishness of God is wiser than human wisdom" (1 Corinthians 1:20, 1:23, 1:25).

For Christians, the ultimate wisdom, of course, is the folly of the cross.

What are some ways the wisdom of Jesus is in opposition to the wisdom of our day? To what extent have I embraced the folly of the cross?

Jesus, sage of God, fill me with your wisdom.

50 On Wishing

Sometimes wishing is the wings the truth comes true on.
—Frederick Buechner

When I taught high school religion, sometimes a student would ask me, "What if Jesus was a hoax? What if he never even existed? What if there isn't any God, and all this stuff we're learning is one big fat lie? Then what?"

Good questions. They are ones I have asked myself on more than one occasion. In fact, I have also asked, "What if this whole nun thing is wrong? What if my vows—especially celibacy—have all been for naught? Then what?"

I have several ways of responding to that "Then what?" I ask myself, "Well, have you been basically happy believing in Jesus and Christianity?" My answer: Yes! "Have you been basically happy living the life of a nun?" Again, my answer is yes! "Have you brought happiness to others by living a life based on Christian principles?" I believe so. And finally, "What have you lost by believing in Jesus, by embracing Christianity?" Well, I am not sure. I have a hunch I have lost some money. And I know I have lost a lot of time. Just think of all the extra time I would have had if I had never prayed, never gone to church, never read a spiritual book, or never served others.

The point is, of course, we do not know for sure about Jesus or Christianity. If we did, we would have no need for faith. Certainty rules out faith. Furthermore, one reason I stick with Christianity is not because I am absolutely sure it is true, but rather because I have found such happiness and fulfillment in living a life based upon its principles. And I admire the lives of so many other people who have also staked their claim on the Gospel. In addition, I say this: If

Christianity is not true, then I wish with all my heart that it would be true. If Jesus is only a figment of someone's imagination, then what a marvelous figment he is! If his teachings about God's unfailing love for us, charity's universal application (even to one's enemies), goodness' ultimate triumph over evil, and life's final victory over death, are only a story, then what a splendid story it is!

Frederick Buechner has written an intriguing little book entitled *Wishful Thinking: A Theological ABC*. Dubbed "a dictionary for the restless believer," the book is a collection of imaginative and thought-provoking definitions of many traditional Christian terms—such as angels, the cross, idolatry, meditation, and sin. In the book, Beuchner defines wishful thinking like this: "Christianity is mainly wishful thinking. Even the part about Judgment and Hell reflect the wish that somewhere the score is being kept." Then he adds, "Sometimes the Truth is what sets us wishing for it."

I like that sentence. To me it says that our very capacity for wishing comes from God. It is God, Truth itself, who has set our hearts to wishing in the first place. (By the way, we sometimes call this wishing *hope*.) What are we wishing or hoping for? For all kinds of things, like peace, love, harmony, joy, excitement, understanding, meaning. And our very wishing for such things can be the first step toward making them a reality.

It is God, Truth itself, who has set our hearts to wishing in the first place.

What am I wishing for?

God, may I encounter your truth in all my wishes today.

51 On Zeal

Nothing great in the world has ever been accomplished without enthusiasm.
—Georg Hegel

I tend to get excited about things. If I spot a rare bird, I excitedly tell someone about it. If I watch a baseball game, I can barely stay in my seat. If I give a talk, I do so with considerable gusto. This tendency of mine toward exuberance did not go unnoticed by the Jesuits with whom I worked for six years. Whenever I got very excited about something, one of them would say to me, "Melannie, you're gushing again!"

But is gushing such a bad thing? Must exuberance always be curbed? I think not. In fact, exuberance is another gift of the Holy Spirit—only we usually call it zeal. The word *zeal* in Greek means "intense heat." In Hebrew, the word denotes the flush that comes to the face of someone experiencing strong emotion. Unfortunately, the word *zeal* has gotten a bad connotation. For some, it connotes only anger. For others, it conjures up images of religious fanatics who scream dire predictions on street corners, shove leaflets into your face at airports, or (worse yet) bomb abortion clinics.

But zeal can be good. Consider this ancient story from the Desert Fathers. Abbot Lot went to see Abbot Joseph and said, "Father, according as I am able, I keep my little rule, and my little fast, my prayer, meditation, and contemplative silence. And according as I am able, I strive to cleanse my heart of bad thoughts. Now what more should I do?" The elder rose up in reply and stretched out his hands to heaven, and his fingers became like lamps of fire. He said, "Why not become all flame?"

Zeal is about "becoming all flame." It is about being on fire with God's love. If we page through Scripture, we find numerous individuals who were zealous and exuberant, who became all flame.

Take David. When David became king of Israel, he comported himself in a kingly, dignified manner—most of the time. But when the Ark of the Covenant was brought to Jerusalem, David was so happy he couldn't control his exuberance (2 Samuel 6). Hearing the horns, harps, and cymbals, he ran out of the palace, whipped off his crown, threw off his kingly robes, and danced with abandon in the streets with the people. We can picture him jumping up and down, swaying back and forth, laughing and singing—in little more than his underwear. As David danced with joy in the street, his wife Michal watched in disgust from a window. In fact, she became furious with David—so much so that she "despised him in her heart."

When David returned to the palace later that day, he was confronted by his raging wife who cried out, "How could you do such a thing?! Dancing like that—in only your shorts! You made a fool of yourself before all the people, you idiot!" (That's a very free translation.) But David replied, "What do you mean, woman? I was dancing before the Ark of the Lord! And I will continue to make merry before the Lord any time I want to! So there!" (Another free translation.)

Comportment has its place, yes. But, when it comes to expressing our love for God and passing on our faith, zeal and exuberance have their place, too. There are times we must resist the pressure to behave, to keep our voices down, to sit quietly in our place. Instead, we must let ourselves be carried away by the joy of knowing that the One who is mighty has done marvelous things for us! Let's dance!

Have I ever met anyone who was "all flame"? How exuberant am I when expressing and passing on my faith?

Exuberant Spirit, grace me with the gift of zeal today!

52 On Death

*Death is not extinguishing the light, it is putting out the lamp
because the dawn has come.*
—Rabindranath Tagore

When I served six years as provincial of the Sisters of Notre Dame, I officiated at the funerals of over sixty sisters. For some of these sisters, I was actually present when they died. For all of them, I wrote and delivered a funeral eulogy. During that time my father also died. I was with him when he breathed his last. Two and a half years later, my mother died. Once again I was by her side. Eight months later, my brother John died of cancer. I was at his bedside too. I guess you could say I am very familiar with death. This familiarity has made death very real for me. It has also underscored for me death's innate mystery.

Death is the ultimate mystery of life. It is absolute, it is final. What adds to its mystery is the fact that no one really knows what happens after death. No one. The way I see it, there are basically two possibilities: Either life goes on after death or life ends. Period. Either our souls are capable of transcending the limits of this earthly life in some way, or our lives are restricted to life here on earth. We Christians choose to believe in life after death. It is a belief rooted in Scripture—more specifically in the resurrection of Jesus from the dead.

Despite our belief that death is the doorway into eternal life, we sometimes think of death in only negative terms. As such, we can be terrorized by death. To have some fear of death is only human, only natural. Remember, in Gethsemane, Jesus himself was terrorized by his impending crucifixion and death. But sometimes our fear of death leads to our denial of death. We refuse to think or talk about death, we put off writing a will, we avoid doctors and hospitals, or we make decisions as if we were going to live on earth forever. To deny the reality of our death is ironic, because our death is the only infallibly certain event in our futures.

Death is a gift of the Holy Spirit. How? Death shows us the preciousness of our days. Time is made more valuable simply because it is finite. Death also shows us what's important in life. It helps to put things in perspective. In the face of death, a little arthritis or a bruised ego is inconsequential, holding grudges is senseless, working only to amass material goods is foolish.

> *Death shows us the preciousness of our days. Time is made more valuable simply because it is finite.*

The poet Carlos Castaneda calls death a wise advisor. He writes that when you have a difficult decision to make, the only sane thing to do is to "turn to your left and ask advice from your death."

How familiar am I with death? If my death is a wise advisor, what is it telling me?

Risen Jesus, strengthen my belief in death as the doorway into eternal life with you and with all of my loved ones.

Bibliography

Bausch, William J. *A World of Stories for Preachers and Teachers: And All Who Love Stories That Move and Challenge.* Mystic, CT: Twenty-Third Publications, 1998.

Bender, Sue. *Everyday Sacred: A Woman's Journey Home.* San Francisco: HarperSanFrancisco, 1996.

Borg, Marcus J. *Meeting Jesus Again for the First Time: The Historical Jesus and the Heart of Contemporary Faith.* New York: HarperCollins, 1995.

Buechner, Frederick. *Wishful Thinking: A Theological ABC.* New York: Harper & Row, 1973.

Burghardt, Walter. *Seasons That Laugh or Weep: Musings on the Human Journey.* New York: Paulist Press, 1983.

Ciardi, John. *The Collected Poems of John Ciardi.* Fayetteville, AK: University of Arkansas Press, 1997.

De Mello, Anthony, SJ. *Taking Flight: A Book of Story Meditations.* New York: Doubleday, 1988.

Dillard, Annie. *The Writing Life.* New York: Harper & Row, 1990.

Farrell, Edward. *Surprised by the Spirit.* Denville, NJ: Dimension Books, 1973.

Green, Thomas H., SJ. *Weeds Among the Wheat: Discernment, Where Prayer and Action Meet.* Notre Dame, IN: Ave Maria Press, 1984.

Hample, Stuart, and Eric Marshall. *Children's Letters to God.* New York: Workman Publishing Company, 1991.

Heschel, Abraham. *I Asked for Wonder: A Spiritual Anthology.* Edited by Samuel H. Dresner. New York: Crossroad, 1983.

Keating, Thomas. *Intimacy with God.* New York: Crossroad, 1994.

Krisher, James A. *Spiritual Surrender: Yielding Yourself to a Loving God.* Mystic, CT: Twenty-Third Publications, 1997.

Lamott, Anne. *Bird by Bird: Some Instructions on Writing and Life.* New York: Doubleday, 1994.

———. *Operating Instructions: A Journal of My Son's First Year.* New York: Pantheon Books, 1993.

Léon-Dufour, Xavier. *Dictionary of the New Testament.* San Francisco: Harper & Row, 1980.

Lewis, C. S. *A Grief Observed.* New York: Seabury Press, 1976.

Marty, Martin, and Micah Marty. *When True Simplicity Is Gained: Finding Spiritual Clarity in a Complex World.* Grand Rapids, MI: William B. Eerdmans Publishing Company, 1998.

McBrien, Richard, gen. ed. *Encyclopedia of Catholicism.* San Francisco: HarperCollins, 1995.

McKenzie, John, SJ. *Dictionary of the Bible.* Milwaukee: Bruce Publishing Company, 1965.

Moore, Thomas. *Care of the Soul: A Guide for Cultivating Depth and Sacredness in Everyday Life.* New York: HarperPerennial, 1994.

Morneau, Robert. *Fathoming Bethlehem: Advent Meditations.* New York: Crossroad, 1997.

Norris, Kathleen. *Amazing Grace: A Vocabulary of Faith.* New York: Riverhead Books, 1999.

Padovano, Anthony. *Who Is Christ?* Notre Dame, IN: Ave Maria Press, 1967.

Paton, Alan. *For You Departed.* New York: Charles Scribner's Sons, 1969.

Pieper, Josef. *Leisure: The Basis of Culture.* New York: Mentor Books, 1952.

Senior, Donald, CP. *Jesus: A Gospel Portrait.* Dayton, OH: Pflaum Press, 1975.